s this is "an essay in applied social philosophy."
gensteinian tradition and follows much of the
ampshire on thought and action.   The author
out being able to say anything substantive
conditions.   His major aim is to analyze
pose their fullest meanings.   He accom-
bly and shows that in spite of his denial
knowledgeable about and sensitive to
the philosopher's basic task as
bad.   This work shows how
n index, a serious draw-
traditional disciplinary
tantial holdings in

Community and ideology

an essay in applied social philosophy

The International Library of Welfare and Philosophy

General Editors

Professor Noel Timms
School of Applied Social Studies,
University of Bradford

David Watson
Department of Moral Philosophy,
University of Glasgow

Community and ideology

an essay in applied social philosophy

Raymond Plant

*Department of Philosophy,
University of Manchester*

Routledge & Kegan Paul
London and Boston

First published in 1974
by Routledge & Kegan Paul Ltd
Broadway House, 68-74 Carter Lane,
London EC4V 5EL and
9 Park Street,
Boston, Mass. 02108, USA
Set in Monotype Times
and printed in Great Britain by
The Lavenham Press Ltd, Lavenham Suffolk, England
© Raymond Plant 1974

ISBN 0 7100 7856 0 (c)
ISBN 0 7100 7857 9 (p)
Library of Congress Catalog Card No. 74-75859

For my parents

Contents

Preface

This book is concerned with an analysis of 'community' as a social and political ideal but it differs somewhat from the usual essay in conceptual analysis because it is concerned with 'community' primarily as it enters into community work, organisation and development. It is thus an attempt at *applied* social philosophy. My use of the notion of ideology in the essay is very much indebted to an article, 'Fact, value and ideology', by A. Montefiore in *British Analytical Philosophy* edited by B. Williams and A. Montefiore, and to the overall inspiration of Stuart Hampshire's *Thought and Action*. I should like to thank the editors of this series for their help, and in particular my thanks are due to Professor Noel Timms who in 1969 supported my first venture in this field with his decision to include my *Social and Moral Theory in Casework* in his Library of Social Work.

Philosophy and social work may not appear on the face of it to have much in common, but earlier in this century they had close contact through the work of the Idealists, and I have to thank Professor Michael Oakeshott for reminding me of this during the course of a Ph.D. oral (on another different subject). I hope, in the not too distant future, to examine these connexions as they appear in the writings of Bosanquet, Green, Jones, Hetherington, etc.

As usual my thanks are due to my wife and children for bearing with my preoccupations and to my friend and colleague, Dr Geraint Parry, for many conversations on the topic of community.

R.P.

There are some concepts which are permanently and essentially subject to question and revision, in the sense that the criteria of their application are always in dispute and are recognised to be at all times questionable.

Stuart Hampshire, *Thought and Action*

1 Philosophy and community work

Rootlessness is by far the most dangerous disease of society.
Simone Weil, *The Need for Roots*

'Community' is crucial to our social and political understanding but, at the same time, it is an elusive concept defying attempts at clear cut analysis. This has not, however, prevented 'community' from becoming something of a vogue word in social description at the present time: community action; community politics; community studies; community organisation; community development; community school; community church; community mental health and even community television are all part of contemporary sociological, educational, theological and political thought and experience. In all of these areas of study and action the elusive concept of community defines and specifies the thought and the activity in question.

At the same time terms which are usually taken to stand at the opposite pole to that of community, with its emphasis upon rootedness, cohesion and belonging, are part of the stock in trade of cultural Jeremiahs on both the left and the right: alienation; estrangement; anomie; rootlessness; loss of attachment are all, we are so often told, part of the crisis of modern mass society. Salvation and redemption are to be found in community; but what is it?

In this book we shall be concerned with the notion of community primarily in so far as it is related to community work, community development and community organisation. At the same time, the concept of community which specifies and individuates community work from other social work activities does not exist in an isolated and dislocated fashion, independent of the perspectives which we have on community elsewhere. Indeed, however far fetched it may seem at this juncture, it will be part of the thesis of this book that the notion of community used in these social work contexts in fact

has its roots in a disposition of thought about society which origina-
ted at the *end of the eighteenth century.*

What specifies this book as a work of philosophy is its analytical
approach to the subject, concerned to elucidate the meaning of
'community' and related concepts. Not so long ago a reader con-
sulting a work on the philosophy of a subject, whether it be education
or politics, art or history, would have expected to find either arguments in favour of certain high level general directives which would
guide practitioners in these particular spheres, or would have found
merely a catalogue of uplifting ideals. Certainly common usage still
preserves such a conception of philosophy in, for instance the,
phrase 'philosophy of life'. However, such a view of philosophy, at
least so far as the Anglo-Saxon tradition is concerned, has virtually
disappeared. Now the emphasis is much more on conceptual analysis
or conceptual exploration—the attempt to explicate the pre-
suppositions and descriptions embodied in a pattern of human
activity and endeavour, whether it be mathematics or social work,
art or history.

Against the earlier rather élitist view of the philosopher both the
hard headed and the sceptical scored a point when they argued that
the philosopher, operating in the empirical vacuum of his study,
has nothing at all to contribute to any understanding of a first order
body of knowledge or activity. Such an objection has obvious force,
but virtually no philosopher would at the present time see the role
of his activity in terms of attempts to issue directives and to formulate
ideals *vis-a-vis* a pattern of activity to which he has only an external
relationship. On the contrary, his role is much more second order
and parasitic. He is concerned far more with the *elucidation* of
concepts and ideas connected to such first order pursuits—in this
particular case the idea of community. He is not concerned with
competing with the social scientist in trying to discover data concerning the distribution of community power, for example, but
with trying to understand what the sociologist, the politically
committed, the social worker and men in the street *mean* when they
talk about 'community'.

This does not entail that the philosophical task is wholly descriptive
—on the contrary. If the philosopher sees inconsistencies and
obscurities in the way in which a body of theory is articulated then,
of course, he has a right to appraise and evaluate such a body of
theory in the light of these discoveries. However, this critical task,

should it be deemed necessary, must wait upon a patient attempt to penetrate and get to know from the inside that body of theory which has attracted the philosopher's interest. Only when he is versed in it, has seen its point, has attempted to explain its character from the inside, is the philosopher in a position to make evaluative and critical comment upon it. Evaluation and criticism are the evaluation and criticism of *something*, something with an identity and a character. It is only in so far as the philosopher has established the identity of a theory from within, as it were, that his evaluation and criticism can have any cutting edge at all.

The motivation of the philosopher in considering the theoretical self-understanding of a form of human activity such as community work, organisation, action and development, if it is not to be merely academic curiosity, must in some way or other be to spread some kind of enlightenment, self consciousness and self knowledge. His purpose must be to follow through implications, see connexions, probe assertions about values and elucidate the grounds of ideas— tasks which are very often neglected by the busy practitioners of the activity whose theoretical dimensions the philosopher explores. His aim is not so much to solve any of the outstanding practical difficulties within, in our case, community work, as to spread an awareness among those involved of the kind of language, its grammar, its logic and its implications which the community worker uses to describe to himself and communicate to others the point of his activity. In this context the analysis will be concerned with community and a cluster of concepts around it—action, locality, participation, interest, norms, etc., to determine their meaning and the pattern of their interrelationships. Of course, many may be impatient with such a philosophical analysis—it deals with *mere* words, concerned with linguistic niceties, grammatical and semantic rectitude, and the natural temptation of the social worker, faced with pressing and urgent problems, to dismiss as unimportant a philosophical approach to his subject may be very great—the kind of irritation which beset Marx when he argued in his *Theses on Feuerbach* that philosophers have only interpreted the world, the task, however, is to change it. It is nevertheless a temptation which needs to be vigorously resisted because it is based upon a fundamentally mistaken view of the relation of theory to practice. There is a tendency to assume that activities and the language used in their description are only externally related—that they are separate and separable things. On such an assumption those who are of a practical rather than a theoretical cast of mind can thus be spared the effort of attending too closely to the theoretical and conceptual discussion of their activities. Such a picture of the relation of theory to practice is mistaken.

Activities and human actions generally are only identified and specified through a system of concepts. A pattern of determinate activity is only what it is in so far as it is described, identified and conceived in a particular way, according to social and linguistic rules, standards and conventions. Actions do not exist as 'brute facts' in the world but are mediated through descriptions. The sheer physical movements of a person's body whether he be engaged in making love or war only constitute those particular actions because certain descriptions are brought to bear. Actions, as opposed to sheer bodily movements, in a very real sense embody ideas and concepts and only in so far as they do are they defined, specified and individuated. In consequence, to examine philosophically a set of concepts relating to a particular mode of human activity is not to examine a mere epiphenomenon of that activity, a detachable and unimportant part, but rather to examine that activity itself from a particular point of view. To give an account of the meaning of a word is to describe how it is used; and to describe how it is used is to describe the mode of social intercourse into which it enters. This applies to the notion of community generally and to community work in particular. The philosopher examining the nexus of concepts surrounding the notion of community is thereby examining an integral part of that particular social practice.

From the point of view of the community worker there are less abstract gains too. In this context the philosopher is concerned to discuss primarily the meaning of 'community' which after all specifies and picks out this particular aspect of social work from the whole of social work. Presumably then, some awareness of what is involved in the notion of community is a gain. As John Stuart Mill said in another context (1910), p. 2:

All action is for the sake of some end and the rules of action it seems natural to suppose must take their whole character and colour from the end to which they are subservient. When we engage in a pursuit, a clear and precise conception of what we are pursuing would seem to be the first thing that we need instead of the last thing we are to look forward to.

The same is true *mutatis mutandis* of the practice of community work. The principles and practical techniques of community work are coloured by and given point by the notion of community which here is precisely the object of philosophical analysis. This point has been well made by Ray Lees (1972, p. 99) when in commenting on Timms (1968) he says:

> As Timms has commented on social workers, 'like students of social administration they have often espoused a cause when they should have attempted to explore a meaning'. Political philosophy has an important contribution to offer this kind of exploration. It can make clear the value assumptions hidden in notions of community, of social improvement and participation, pinpointing important ethical considerations.

Finally, from the point of view of the philosopher and the community worker there are gains to be had in the philosophical treatment of the activity. From the philosopher's point of view there is a body of theory intrinsically related to an important social function in our society to be elucidated which is moreover concerned in a practical way with an important area of traditional philosophical controversy, namely the general relationship of the individual to society. By the same token, however, because the community worker is so involved in evaluative judgmetns about the need to develop a particular quality and type of social experience—that covered in a shorthand way by the word 'community'—he may well find philosophical discussion helpful in that similar kinds of judgments about the desirable character of social experience have often been made and defended by a large number of social and moral philosophers. Indeed, this very point is echoed in Younghusband (1968, p. 115) when the members of the committee indicated what they considered to be the most important components in the training of community workers:

> Their tasks in intervening in the human situation, their interest in social change, their concern with social dysfunction as they and their agencies see it mean that social philosophy becomes an important frame of reference....Examination of values is therefore essential to the teachina of government, politics and social administration and above gll in the teaching of the

principles and practice of community work where the focus
moves from academic discussion to principles and methods of
action.

This book should be seen as an attempt to contribute in a small
way to the fulfilment of this need which is not, as it were, 'wished
onto' busy practitioners by the philosopher but, as the above
quotation makes clear, arises naturally when community workers
reflect on the question of the justification of their own activity.

One final point might be made at this juncture. It might well be
thought that philosophical interest in social work generally, and
work in the community in particular, is a new and indeed rather an
exiguous phenomenon. Such a view would, however, reveal an
ignorance of both the history of philosophy and of social work. In
the later years of the nineteenth century, and in the early years of
this, a good many philosophers were theoretically interested in and
indeed actively engaged in social work of all kinds. This was largely
a result of the influence of the moral and political theorising of
Thomas Green who was for some time White's Professor of Moral
Philosophy at Oxford. Many of Green's pupils took very seriously
his teaching on the role of the state, the nature of welfare and the
notion of citizenship, and made either practical or theoretical
contributions to social work. Perhaps the most notable of these was
Bernard Bosanquet who was both an important academic social and
political theorist and a well known figure on the Council of the
Charity Organisation Society. He combined these functions on
occasion and produced several contributions to the philosophical
understanding of social work aims and methods, particularly *Three
Lectures on Social Ideals* (1917a), *Politics and Charity* (1917b) and
Philosophy and Casework (1917c). Indeed, his major general work on
social and political philosophy, *The Philosophical Theory of the
State* (1923), a book incidentally dedicated to Charles Loch of the
Charity Organisation Society, may still be read with interest and
profit by social workers, an observation which is particularly true for
community workers in relation to his chapter on 'Institutions as
ethical ideals', with its sensitive discussion of the neighbourhood
community. Indeed, Bosanquet was so convinced of the relation of
philosophical understanding to practice that he prefaced his book
with the remark that the work of the social reformer should no more
be regarded as an appendix to social theory than the work of the
doctor is regarded as a mere appendix to physiology. In his *Non-*

Directive Approach in Group and Community Work (1967, p. 9),
T. R. Batten says of the rise of community work:

> Community work in its modern sense in Britain was begun in
> the 19th century by upper and middle class idealists and
> reformers who sought to articulate the often appalling con-
> ditions in which the working class people lived in the new
> industrial towns.

Many such reformers acted in this way because of what they had
learned from the teaching of Green and Bosanquet.

Since this time, however, both philosophy and social work have
developed in their own directions. Philosophers became more
interested in logic and epistemological problems and less concerned
with social and political thought (see Plant in Cox and Dyson, 1972,
vol. II, ch. 4); social work, on the other hand, has tried to find a base
more secure than the shifting sands of philosophy and has found it
in this or that psychological theory usually of a Freudian type.
However, in more recent times the philosophical climate has become
more amenable to broader interests (see Plant in Cox and Dyson,
1972, vol. III, ch. 2) and at the same time social workers have become
disenchanted with the too individualistic perspective offered by
Freudian theory, and have tried to relate their client's problems far
more to the community at large, and in doing so have been forced
to raise fundamental questions about the nature of society. Whereas
Bosanquet, for example, was concerned to provide some specifically
philosophical basis for social work, the present author is concerned
with a less ambitious undertaking, namely to explore the kinds of
bases which social and, in particular, community workers offer for
their own activity. It may be that these bases need revision, but it is
up to the practitioners to change if they feel it necessary but perhaps
drawing upon some of the points made in this book and from
traditional philosophical theorising about the nature of community.

2 Community as fact and value

> All Community work is shot through with assumptions that some forms of social life and change are better than others.
> Younghusband, 1968, p. 77

Dimensions of meaning

It is a very common error to think that if a word is meaningful then it should have a fixed and wholly determinate meaning and, further, that its meaning should be in just one mode—that the word should have only one use, for example a descriptive function. An example of this view would be that all meaningful words in fact stand as names designating objects, however loosely 'object' may be construed. On such a basis the word 'community' would stand as a name denoting some determinate object, namely a particular *type* of social life and experience. To elucidate the meaning of community would be equivalent to determining *that* feature of a nexus of social practices to which the word 'community' refers, and it would then follow that this feature of social life, once determined, would then act, as it were, as the 'object', in the loose sense indicated, to which the word 'community' refers. It would also follow that if the word was to be used meaningfully then this feature, this 'object', would have to be present on all occasions of its use. All communities, on such a view, must then share a common factor and the presence of this factor secures the meaning of 'community' when it is ascribed to a particular form of social life.

Usually, no doubt, we think that such words refer to palpable objects—for example, a pushchair, a table or whatever—and there might, for this reason, be some questions about how we might determine that feature of social life to which the word 'community' refers. A good many of the candidates for this feature, for example, a sense of belonging, sense of identity, shared values, etc., are not palpably detectable traits of social life in any straightforward sense.

However, this might be regarded as only a *technical* difficulty about giving some acceptable operational or behavioural definition to these notions and, assuming this to be possible, and there is no *a priori* reason for thinking it to be impossible, then the general view of how to approach the elucidation of the meaning of 'community' could still be adopted.

It is arguable, however, that such a view of meaning and the consequent search for a common factor to act as the meaning of the word is misconceived, at least as a total view of the meaning of 'meaning'. To regard all meaningful words as names, as having a wholly referential character, is mistaken. It involves on the one hand torturing some perfectly ordinary words upon a procrustean bed in order to make them yield meanings of the requisite logical type; on the other hand, the meaning, when so produced, often does not do justice to the varieties of uses which the word may have in ordinary discourse. This opposition to the persuasive name-object view of meaning was argued very forcibly by Ludwig Wittgenstein in his later writings. In his earlier *Tractatus Logico-Philosophicus* Wittgenstein took it for granted that words function as names standing for objects, but in his later *Philosophical Investigations* he vigorously rejected his own earlier view. To illustrate the point of his attack upon the received notion of meaning he took a specific example— the word 'game'. On the received view, such a word would have to be construed as referring to a kind of object, that is to say that feature which all games share. But, Wittgenstein argues, this view is sheer prejudice and cannot account for the ways in which we actually employ the word in perfectly normal situations. On this issue he says (trans. G. E. M. Anscombe, 1958, para. 66):

> Consider for example the proceedings that we call 'games'. I mean board-games, card-games, ball-games, Olympic games, and so on. What is common to them all?—Don't say: 'There *must* be something common, or they would not be called "games" '—but *look and see* whether there is anything common to all. For if you look at them you will not see something that is common to *all*, but similarities, relationships, and a whole series of them at that. To repeat: don't think, but look! Look for example at board-games, with their multifarious relationships. Now pass to card-games; here you find many correspondences with the first group, but many common features drop out, and others appear. When we pass next to ball-games, much that is

common is retained, but much is lost.—Are they all 'amusing'? Compare chess with noughts and crosses. Or is there always winning and losing, or competition between players? Think of patience. In ball-games there is winning and losing; but when a child throws his ball at the wall and catches it again, this feature has disappeared. Look at the parts played by skill and luck; and at the difference between the skill in chess and skill in tennis. Think now of games like ring-a-ring-a-roses; here is the element of amusement, but how many other characteristic features have disappeared? And we can go through the many, many other groups of games in the same way; can see how similarities crop up and disappear.

It is very difficult, Wittgenstein argues, to hold, once the evidence is considered, that the meaningful use of a word in a variety of cases absolutely requires that there should be one feature in common. As he says in *The Blue and Brown Books* (trans. G. E. M. Anscombe, 1969, p. 19):

> The idea that in order to get clear about the meaning of a general term one had to find the common element in all its applications has shackled philosophical investigation; for it has not only led to no result, but also made the philosopher dismiss as irrelevant the concrete cases which alone could have helped him to understand the usage of the term.

If we reject the idea that a word *must* stand for some kind of object—that which all things designated by the word share—then we shall become more open in our attitude towards language. Freed from the preconception of essentialism we shall no longer be preoccupied with looking at language in a one-dimensional way, that is to say looking for *the* meaning of a word, but we shall on the contrary be more alive to the 'open texture' of its use—its actual use in language and thought, in the description, interpretation, organisation and evaluation of behaviour.

Such a change in perspective does not, however, mean that one cannot bring any general considerations to bear on the grammar of a particular word—its use, implications and status. Indeed, such a general point might be made at this juncture, one which will prove to be of great value in our analysis of 'community'—that is to draw a distinction between descriptive meaning and evaluative meaning, or the use of a word to describe some object or state of affairs and the use of a word to evaluate and to commend it. Although at first sight these two general forms of usage may well appear mutually exclusive, they are not so in practice because a word may, on a particular occasion of its use, embody both descriptive and evaluative elements. Two examples might make this clear.

The words 'Fascist' and 'Democratic' are in reasonably common usage in our political vocabulary but even a very cursory examination of their use reveals general lessons which we shall find illuminating in the context of 'community'. To call a person or a party 'Fascist' is certainly in some way or other, however obliquely, to refer to some feature of the person's behaviour or the policy of the party. The totality of these features—for example, belief in certain economic and racial doctrines, a view of the state as a spiritual entity coupled with a belief in the virtues of discipline and militarism, and involving a contempt for democratic procedures—may be regarded as con- stituting the complex range of descriptive meaning of 'Fascist'. But, at the same time, to call a person or a party Fascist is not *just* a descriptive use of language, however complex. It is *ipso facto* to evaluate it, to place it in a particular moral light and to invite dis- approval for either the person or the policy of the party. Certainly 'Fascist' has a descriptive meaning but equally clearly it has had, in this country at least, since the 1930s for the majority of people a strong pejorative force. In this particular case within the one word we are able to distinguish, after the most cursory glance at its usage, two distinct dimensions of meaning—a descriptive and an evaluative one. Merely to take the view that the word 'Fascist' refers to some *particular* political attitude which all Fascists share is not wholly mistaken, but it does ignore the *complexity* of its descriptive meaning and, more importantly, it neglects its *evaluative* dimension altogether.

Very similar points may be made about the use of 'democracy'. When people use 'democratic' to characterise institutions they do use the word perhaps to refer obliquely to a wide set of detectable traits in that institution, for example the degree of its accountability, the level of its participation and the openness of its decision making. But at the same time when it is used in this way it encapsulates a set of favourable attitudes. Democracy is widely regarded as a 'good thing'. People, governments and nations do not care to be labelled undemocratic and in consequence we have the rather singular situation in which countries of widely different, and indeed often opposed, political systems like to be able to call themselves democratic. It is perhaps useful to quote at this juncture the words of a prominent political scientist (Crick, 1964, p. 6):

> Democracy is perhaps the most promiscuous word in the world of public affairs. She is everybody's mistress and yet retains her value even when a lover sees her favours in his light illicitly shared by many another.

Crick's point is not purely formal. In 1949 UNESCO sponsored an enquiry into the ideals associated with the concept of democracy, and from this enquiry two major points emerged:

A   There were *no* replies hostile to democracy
B   The idea of democracy was considered to be highly ambiguous.
    (UNESCO, 1951.)

Both of these points go to uphold the general issue argued in this section, namely that some words have a very strong evaluative meaning and that when they do the descriptive meaning may well become contested or at least vague and open to many interpretations. What is *the* descriptive meaning of 'democracy' when both the USA and East Germany claim to be democracies?

The basis of the whole problem may be seen when paradigm cases of descriptive and evaluative meaning are contrasted. 'Pushchair' is a word with a wholly descriptive meaning, the meaning which it has is clear and it refers to a determinate type of object. 'Good' on the other hand has no descriptive meaning at all when taken in isolation. When both the descriptive and evaluative dimensions of meaning come together, as is the case with both 'Fascist' and 'Democracy', and, it will be argued, with 'Community', then the descriptive meanings of these words become highly problematic and highly contested. Their descriptive meanings, unlike the case of 'Pushchair', are highly complex and from within this complexity certain aspects of the meaning of 'Fascist', 'Democracy' or 'Community' are selected, depending upon the general value position or ideology of the person or group concerned. It is often argued that community is very difficult to define, but this is in the nature of the case. Its descriptive meaning is already complex (it need not be regarded as unitary and one dimensional if Wittgenstein's argument about games is borne in mind) and from within this complexity *certain* features are emphasised depending upon the value position of the person concerned. 'Community' is so much a part of the stock in trade of social and political argument that it is unlikely that some non-ambiguous and non-contested definition of the notion can be given. The points made here programmatically will now be discussed in more detail.

'Community' and the dimensions of meaning

> The 'pure' model against which all conceivable communities
> could be compared is the proverbial will-o'-the-wisp.
> R. C. Wood, *Suburbia*

It has been argued in what has gone before that the analysis fits the case of community. That it has a wide descriptive meaning, as has 'game', and that it also has an evaluative dimension, and that from this particular evaluative standpoint some aspects of the descriptive meaning of community are emphasised at the expense of others.

The fact that community has some sort of descriptive meaning cannot really be doubted. That is to say it is not used in a *wholly* evaluative way, but having said this the range of its descriptive meaning is very wide, and indeed some features which have been held to be definitive of community by different theorists may well be incompatible. Community has been linked to locality, to identity of functional interests, to a sense of belonging, to shared cultural and ethnic ideas and values, to a way of life opposed to the organisation and bureaucracy of modern mass society, etc.—a whole nexus of traits some of which may well turn out, on analysis, to be incompatible. The descriptive meaning of community is at least as complex as that of 'game'.

The evaluative dimension of the word is more difficult to illustrate precisely largely because the whole notion of evaluative meaning is considerably less clear cut than that of descriptive meaning. Perhaps the first point to be made in the discussion though, partly in the author's self-defence, is that social scientists themselves and community workers do seem to be aware that 'community' is a word and a concept fraught with normative import. In an introduction to a volume of readings the editors, one a sociologist, the other a political scientist, comment (Minar and Greer, 1969, p. 9):

> Community is both empirically descriptive of a social structure
> and normatively toned. It refers both to the unit of society as it
> is and to the aspects of that unit that are valued if they exist
> and desired in their absence.

Similarly in a very useful volume, Bell and Newby (1972, p. 21) argue:

Most sociologists seem to have weighed in with their own idea of what a community consists of and in this lies much of the confusion. For sociologists no more than other individuals have not been immune to the emotive overtones that the word community constantly carries with it. Everyone—even sociologists—has wanted to live in a community; feelings have been more equivocal concerning life in collectivities, networks and societies. The subjective feelings that the term community conjures up thus leads to a confusion between what is (empirical description), and what the sociologists felt it should be (normative prescription).

It will be part of the argument of this book that this is not, as Bell and Newby seem to imply, something which may be avoided but rather something in the nature of the case with a contested notion like 'community' with its complex descriptive dimension.

To talk about community is therefore to talk in two different dimensions—the descriptive and the evaluative—and, because 'community' is intrinsically involved in discussion about the proper nature of social organisation, that is to say what society ought to be like, its descriptive meaning becomes contested as well as complex. Mann (1965) comments that the word community 'has a high level of use but a low level of meaning' and we may, at this juncture, interpret this as implying that one cannot clearly distinguish between meaning and use—to talk about *the* meaning of a word often neglects its complexity and the variety of its uses, and that 'community' has a very strong evaluative use which has a very great influence upon the selection of the descriptive content of the word. This, it has been suggested, is in the nature of the case when one word embodies both a descriptive and an evaluative dimension. Bearing this point in mind we must regard the following comment by Richard Hillery (1968, p. 4) as both utopian and mistaken:

> The moral to be drawn is a scientific one: our definitions must be wedded to facts—those things which are perceived through the senses. The error which is often made in the definition of concepts of community is what may be referred to as the sin of pronouncement. Students have pronounced upon the traits they felt should be contained in community and then have proceeded to look at the facts.

This assertion is utopian in that it neglects the ubiquitous and non-detachable nature of the evaluative element in the notion of community and that the evaluative position of those operating with the notion may well determine the aspect of the descriptive meaning of community to be emphasised. It is mistaken in that it really is intolerably naive to think that community is to be regarded as a 'fact perceived through the senses' (whatever that may mean). It is, on the contrary, a very complex and contested interpretation which we place upon our social experience.

What is the source of the evaluative meaning of community? Why has it come to have this intrinsic evaluative dimension to its use? We can reasonably well understand why 'Fascist' and 'Democracy' have a very high evaluative content; wars have been fought ostensibly to overcome the one and to strengthen the other, but why is it that community has come to have its prescriptive, normative force? In the same way as we have to look at history and tradition to see the source of the evaluative dimensions of 'Fascist' and 'Democracy' so we have to look at the history of social and political thought and experience to see the grounds and the nature of the evaluative side of community. As Bell and Newby claim in the study cited above (1972, p. 21): 'The normative character of community can be related to the history of sociology itself.' An understanding of this history is not therefore something detachable and peripheral, which the community worker may do without; it is rather a central way in which the evaluative meaning of 'community', a word defining his own activity, can be understood.

Community as a value in the sociological tradition

As Bell and Newby argue, the answer to the question of why community has the evaluative force that it has, is to be found by looking at the perspectives on community formulated by some of those thinkers who have been central in forming the sociological tradition. Clearly this is a task which could well merit a book in its own right and it is in addition a task for which a philosopher is not well suited—it is a task for the historian of ideas. However, if we want to become even moderately clear about the evaluative side to community, which I have suggested rather determines its descriptive meaning, then it is a task which cannot be put off. Consequently, in this section some crude attempt will be made to look at the career of the concept of community within the formation of the sociological tradition. Fortunately a very great deal of the spadework has already been done in this field by Professor Robert Nisbet in his book *The Sociological Tradition* (1967), and more impressionistically in his *The Quest for Community* (1970).

In these two works Nisbet fixes the rise of the idea of community as an important ideal in social and political theory in the late eighteenth and early nineteenth centuries, particularly in the German thought of the period. The rise of the idea during this period has often been described as 'the rediscovery of community' and to put the point in this way invites the questions 'What went before?' 'What was it about what went before which led to the subsequent emphasis upon the notion of community?' 'What was it that was being rediscovered?'

For many of the seminal social theorists of this period in Germany, particularly Herder, Schiller and Hegel, a sense of community had existed paradigmatically in the Greek polis, particularly in Periclean Athens. It was thought that in the polis was to be found a form of social organisation and interaction which went far beyond mere locality. The culture of the polis was regarded as homogeneous, participatory and open to all; religion, politics, art and family life were all intertwined in a close and tightly knit fashion, and the Germans took this over-idealised image of the Greek city state as a paradigm in terms of which they could criticise the atrophied and enervated character of social life in western Europe. Indeed this image of community derived from the Greeks has been pervasive in Western social thought and in two recently published books on the analysis of the notion of community the authors have felt constrained to include some discussion of the Greek city state. These discussions are to be found in Minar and Greer cited above, and in René König (1968). As the Germans took their ideal of community from Greek culture it was felt that this reality of the homogeneous, participatory, rooted community had been lost sight of in the modern world. In the following sections an attempt will be made to specify more fully the nature of this community ideal and the reasons which were given to account for its loss in modern life.

Community and the whole man

It was widely felt by the Germans that the idea of community involved some notion of the whole man, in which men were to be met by other men in the totality of their social roles and not in a fragmented or segmental way. All interactions within a community take place within a web of inclusive ties—men are related to one another through more than one description. The modern world however with its progressive division of labour and the development of mass urban society had destroyed the idea of the whole man. In modern society man was now a narrow and enervated being and the nature of his social contacts had become more and more fragmented. This was a point made particularly by Schiller in his *Letters on the Aesthetic Education of Man*, written towards the end of the eighteenth century in which he claimed that social contacts had become segmented as a result of the division of labour. This idea that community involves the notion of the whole man and not fragmented forms of human interaction, though connected with certain preconceptions of the German Romantic movement still plays a very major part in the idea of community. It is retained in the idea that community lifts man out of the particularity of his own personal and selfish interests so that in community he is given a less narrow and sectional sort of social experience and this gives force to those who see in community the concrete realisation of fraternity and co-operation. Nisbet (1967, p. 47) has commented upon this idea of the whole man as being something central to the idea of community as it has developed since the nineteenth century: 'Community is founded upon man conceived in his wholeness rather than in one or another of the roles taken separately that he may hold in the social order.' Certainly, part of the decline of the reality of community forms in the modern world has been linked with the loss of this idea of the enveloping nature of social contact, a loss which has been seen as the result of the process of urbanisation. Louis Wirth has argued this point particularly well (1957, p. 54):

Characteristically urbanites meet one another in highly seg-mented roles. They are to be sure dependent upon more people for the satisfaction of their needs than rural people and are thus associated with a greater number of organised groups, but they are less dependent upon particular persons and their dependence upon others is confined to a highly fractionalised aspect of the others' activity.

The same kind of emphasis upon the segmentation of the person in modern urban society compared with the totality of the person in the older communal forms of social organisation is to be found in Harvey Cox (1968, p. 56). He does, however, make the point at once more concretely and graphically than does Wirth:

Now as an urbanite, my transactions are of a very different sort. If I need to have the transmission of my car repaired, buy a television antenna or cash a cheque, I find myself in functional relationships with mechanics, salesmen and bank clerks whom I never see in any other capacity...the relationships are unfaceted and segmental. I meet these people in no other context. To me they remain as essentially anonymous as I do to them.

This connexion between the loss of community and the loss of the reality of total personal contact in the social sphere, though closely related originally to central preoccupations of the German romantics has become part of the moral background within which and against which the notion of community makes sense. It is insisted upon again in one of the most recent studies of the notion of community, in Poplin (1972) in which he argues that members of communities regard each other as whole persons who are of intrinsic significance and worth whereas members of mass society regard each other as means to ends and assign no such intrinsic worth and significance to the individual. In its attempt at the rediscovery of the community the sociological tradition from the nineteenth century is therefore on this view to attempt to recapture some sense of the wholeness of human nature which has been lost sight of in modern mass society. It is this context among others to be discussed which has given the notion of community its singular evaluative dimension.

Community and social divisions

The division of labour did not lead just to the fragmentation of the human personality, the progressive differentiation of function also led to deep social divisions based upon identities of functional interest—the most ubiquitous of these being the development of social classes. Class relationships, so it was thought, divided the previously homogeneous community. If community presupposes shared values and interests, then the development of social classes and interest groups generally within society is inimical to the main-tenance of the reality of community. Rousseau was one of the very first to see that the sectional interests developed as a result of the division of labour are inimical to the development of an homogeneous community and he put the point very succinctly in his *Premier Discours sur les sciences et les arts* (1964 edn, p. 26): 'We have among us physicians, geometers, chemists, astronomers, poets, musicians and painters but we have no citizens.' Marx took the same kind of argument much further, seeing the problem of the fragmentation of society and of the personality as part and parcel of industrial capitalism which replaced the communal virtues of co-operation and fraternity with those of conflict and competition. Capitalism was seen as an isolating and separating process that stripped off the historically grown layers of custom and social membership and replaced these benign features of social life with competition and the cash nexus. The appeal to the values of community has therefore often been at the very same time a critique of industrial capitalism and it is significant that in Marx's mature communist society he envisages that social classes will have disappeared along with economic domination, and in this new community there will be no rigid tying to function. Rousseau, too, in *Le Contrat social* sought a definition of community which he thought could exist only when the sectional interests parasitic upon the division of labour had been stripped away. Thus the notion of community has been used by both conservative and radical critics of industrialism or industrial capitalism to formulate the predicament of man in modern society, and again this use has radically influenced the evaluative dimension of the word.

Community and the loss of political involvement

A further major feature in man's contemporary condition which preoccupied those who formed the sociological tradition of which our present understanding of community is a part, and which indeed has continued to influence contemporary thinking on community, has been the increasing organisation and bureaucratisation of life generally but in particular in the sphere of politics. In a community, so it might be said, a man is and feels an integral part of an overall way of life, he is not conscious of a division between his own attitudes to the community and the way in which that community organises and articulates its life. He is in a full sense a *member* of the community. However, the argument would continue, with the development of the industrial revolution, political, economic and social power has become increasingly centralised and in consequence men have come to feel less and less at home in the social world; they have become estranged from that social world in which they live, move and have their being. Hegel identified this process as early as the decline of the Republican government in Rome but whatever the historical validity of his strictures on Roman society, his comment still sums up a way of thinking about the individual *vis-a-vis* the organisation of modern life (Hegel, ed Nohl, 1907, p. 223):

> The picture of the state as the product of his own energies disappeared from the citizen's soul. The care and the oversight of the whole rested upon one man or a few....Each man's part in the congeries which formed the whole was so inconsiderable in relation to the whole that the individual did not realise this relation or keep it in view.... All activity and every purpose now had a bearing upon something individual—activity was no longer for the sake of the whole or the ideal.

This way of thinking about man and his relationship to the modern state has, since the time of Hegel, become paradigmatic and the notion of community has been used in this context to point the contrast to the impersonality of the large scale organisation whether it be political, economic or social. This use of community in this controversy is not something on which we can turn our backs. Indeed we are in the thick of the same sorts of ideological controversy and we use community in much the same way as the counterpoint to the impersonality of modern life. Again the history of the sociological tradition enables us to appreciate this further source of the evaluative side to community which is still such an intrinsic part of its meaning. Sheldon Wolin (1961, p. 363) has stressed precisely this point, namely the extent to which the theoretical battle-lines today surrounding the notion of community were first laid down in the nineteenth century and thus the social and political thought of that period at least in so far as it concerns community and organisation is still a central part of our social and political thought and understanding:

> The preoccupation with 'society' gave rise to two closely inter-related problems which troubled almost every major writer in the nineteenth century and continues to perplex the present. They are the problems of community and of organisation. Stated in very broad language the thesis is this...the social and political thought of the nineteenth and twentieth centuries has largely centered on the attempt to restate the value of community, that is the need of human beings to dwell in more intimate relationships with each other, to enjoy more affective ties, to experience some closer solidarity than the nature of urbanised and industrialised society seemed willing to grant. At

the same time, the thought of the period followed another
direction, one which presented an obvious threat to the communitarian development. In the words of an older historian, the
nineteenth century was a period saturated with the idea of
organisation. (Compare Younghusband 1968, p. 10.)

Wolin deals with the tension between the communitarian idea and
the pervasiveness of the organisational ethos in general terms but
more often than not this tension was felt most acutely with reference
to the increasingly complex organisation of the political structure
and Nisbet in an article interestingly enough published in the
International Review of Community Development (1960) has stressed
the political dimension to this problem. He argues that the state
cannot provide the individual the sense of rootedness and security
which he needs because 'by its very nature it is too large, too complex
and altogether too aloof from the residual meanings which human
beings live by.' Only some rediscovered reality of community in
modern life will be able to provide the recognition, fellowship,
security and membership which all men crave. This way of thinking
about community, although it has deep historical roots, is still
central. How much of the radical line in community work is inspired
by a sense that social and political institutions in modern life are
too distant, too remote and too bureaucratised to be responsive to
the needs and wants of individuals? Certainly this is largely how one
community work theorist sees the contemporary predicament and
in reading his statement of it we may perhaps recall a point made in
the first chapter, that community work may well be seen as an attempt
to give some kind of practical expression to a way of thinking
about the adequacy of social experience which had its roots in the
nineteenth century. This is how G. F. Thomason sees the situation
(1969, p. 62):

> The urban context is seen as one in which the collective tissue of
> society has been pared away leaving behind a condition of
> individual isolation, apathy, anomie and deregulation...when in
> this sort of way we imply that we are losing our own sense of
> belonging we can expect a purely emotional response to this
> machine of urban civilisation because it denies man the oppor-
> tunity to learn through the community group and to derive
> social and emotional support from the same source. Re-creation
> of the community then becomes the ideal to be aimed for in
> community work.

Again the evaluative dimension of community becomes built in because the idea of community becomes the yardstick by which the atrophied nature of contemporary social reality is judged.

Christianity and community

The final factor which was of importance in this attempt to look again at the idea and reality of community was the problem posed by Christianity. To argue that Christianity should pose a problem for the communitarian ideal may appear somewhat paradoxical because many have seen in Christianity the very paradigm of community. Indeed a recent clerical reviewer of a book on the relationship between the church and community development was moved to declare (*Expository Times*, 1973, No. 5): 'The Bible is a story of community development. It relates accounts of failures, points prophetically to factors which make for good relationships and looks for an eternal city.' But more particularly it might be argued it is in the experience of *Koinonia*, of being part of the body of Christ, that makes the Christian church a paradigm of community.

However, those who were concerned with the divisive features of the Christian faith would pick up the point made in the review above, that the church points towards a *heavenly* city, to try to show that the Christian's concern for community life is not serious. Instead of building up a shared reciprocating community life, the ends of human existence are seen by the Christian to lie outside of and beyond the immediate society of which he is a member. This dimension of Christian teaching was reinforced by some of the church's major teachers and theologians. Following St Peter who argued in his *Epistle* that the Christian is 'an alien in a foreign land', St Augustine formulated his notion of the two loves of the two cities in his major work on social and political theology *De Civitate Dei* and the socially divisive nature of Christianity was well stated by St Thomas Aquinas in *Summa Theologica* (11a, 21, 4): 'Man does not belong to the political community with the whole of his being (secundum se totum) nor with all that he is (secundum se tota sua).' With the general decline of the reality of community as a result of the other factors discussed so far in this chapter many thinkers who wished to stress again the idea of community turned part of their attention to the role of Christianity in contemporary culture. If community rests upon shared values how is Christianity, with its transcendent dimension, going to fit into a rediscovered notion of community in a world which is more and more dominated by a secular ethos? In the nineteenth century this was a problem posed by Hegel, Strauss and Feuerbach and one which was taken up again in this century with specific relationship to the problem of community in the modern world by Bonhoeffer (1961 and 1962); by Harvey Cox (1968), and by Thomas Altizer (1967), closely following Hegel. A good many of the issues here are dealt with more fully in the present author's *Hegel* (1973) and in Alasdair MacIntyre's 'God and the Theologians' (reprinted in MacIntyre, 1972).

This general tradition of theorising about community, many of the forms of which have been only crudely noticed above, reached it greatest expression perhaps in Ferdinand Tönnies's book *Gemeinschaft und Gesellschaft*, published in 1887, (see Tönnies 1955 for the English edition), which was a paean to the lost community and an indictment of the baneful effects of many of the features of contemporary life noted earlier in this chapter. In this work Tönnies, against this evaluative background, preoccupied with the loss of community, tried to work out a typology for on the one hand real interacting reciprocating community, *Gemeinschaft*, and on the other hand the aggregation of individualistic atomistic society, *Gesellschaft*. This typology conceived in the thick of the ideological controversy and social criticism discussed above has dominated thinking about community ever since.

In *Gemeinschaft*, human relationships are intimate, face to face and not discrete and segmented—they are with the whole man, not with a man under a particular description or acting from within a particular role. In such a society the central question of *Gesellschaft*, 'Who are you and with whom do I deal?' cannot arise. Each person knows the others in the round. Because a community shares its values there can be no fundamental moral conflicts, roles and relationships cohere and cannot conflict. The community is stable in that physical mobility between one place and another is not of any importance within this kind of society and there is very little or no mobility in terms of status. The ethic is very much of the 'my station and its duties' type.

On the other hand *Gesellschaft* relationships are characteristic of large scale modern societies and institutions. The dominant image of relationship here is that of contract and not habit or customary observance. The authority of such a society is not traditional, indeed it is based upon the opposite—the legal, rational notions of consent, volition and contract, a view which implies a radically individualistic account of the genesis and authority of the legal order. Kaspar Naegale (1961) has fairly summarised one aspect of Tönnies's distinction, that in terms of the interaction of persons and it can I think be seen in the following quotation the extent to which Tönnies's book, which has become a classic of sociology and from which most modern discussions of community start, is indebted to the works of the German romantics which were really the fountainhead of this disposition of thought about man and society (p. 184):

> Relations of the *Gemeinschaft* type are more inclusive; persons confront each other as ends, they cohere more durably....In *Gesellschaft* their mutual regard is circumscribed by a sense of specific if not formal obligations. A transaction may occur without any other encounters leaving both parties virtually anonymous.

If Tönnies's distinctions are translated into current sociological jargon in terms of primary and secondary groups or in terms of organic and functional relationships we may see how far our contemporary sociological understanding of the community was laid down in the latter part of the nineteenth century in the thick of ideological controversies which still are part of our consciousness.

At the same time, the above analysis may provide too homogeneous an impression. It may seem that all the favourable evaluative attitudes to community were of the same sort within the sociological tradition, whereas they were often very different. Indeed the different nature of these evaluative attitudes helps to bear out a point repeated frequently thus far, namely that the nature of the evaluative attitude or ideology may well determine the aspect of descriptive meaning taken to be paradigm. Some of those who praised community, such as Tönnies, were basically conservatives who used the notion of community to diagnose the baneful effects of contemporary urban industrial society, seeing in the notion of community an encapsulation of the values of the rural community for which they had a considerable degree of nostalgia. Such conservatives took community to refer mainly to locality, to fixed modes and hierarchies of status and power with little physical or social mobility, embodying shared values based upon some shared, traditional way of looking at the world. Such a view of community embodied the static, orderly, rooted notions which were central to conservative thought. In this case the conservative evaluative attitude structured what was held to be central to the descriptive dimension of community. What was counted as central was what cohered with the basic value standpoint. Others, less conservative, such as Hegel and Schiller, fully accepted the values which urban industrial society had realised, freedom to move, a growth in individuality and a wider capacity for consumption, but at the same time they wished to counterbalance these achievements with some reformulated notion of community experience which would negative the more baneful consequences of urban civilisation. Their view of community was not so much nostalgic as progressive and liberal, attempting to assimilate the values of individuality within the notion of community. In doing so Hegel particularly put far less stress upon locality and the sense of belonging to a specific place than the conservatives, but saw the achievement of community in the modern world to depend upon functional groups, which he called Corporations, and upon greater political participation and awareness. Here again what is taken to be central to community is not, as it were, a set of brute facts discoverable outside of a particular framework of evaluation, rather the diminution of the stress upon locality and the increase of emphasis upon shared ends and the extent to which shared values are to be seen as a consequence of functional co-operation were necessitated by a basically progressive or liberal ideological framework. Others again, notably Marx and Rousseau, provided a very radical understanding of community demanding neither a return to a pre-industrial rural ethos nor an attempt to tinker with the social consequences of industrialism. On the contrary, only a fundamental change in social and economic conditions could regenerate those values which *they* took to be central to the idea of community, particularly those of fraternity and co-operation, but fraternity and co-operation based not upon some mutual recognition within a functional specialism but rather based upon some awareness of a common humanity, an awareness distorted by the hierarchical nature of rural community and by the competitiveness of community based upon specialisation of function. Again what is taken to be central to the descriptive meaning of community, namely fraternity and co-operation, is accredited by the ideological position.

Community: the British tradition

So far in this book attention has been paid mainly to continental thinkers—Hegel, Herder, Schiller, Marx, Rousseau and Tönnies, and the understanding of community which we have inherited from them; but this is not to imply that this means that the 'rediscovery of the community' was not a part of British social theory in the nineteenth and the twentieth centuries. Indeed many of the thinkers who provided the raw materials of the initial German reaction were British—Adam Smith, Adam Ferguson, John Millar and Sir James Steuart and they had themselves recognised the decline of the rural community as well as some of the baneful effects of the development of what Adam Smith called the 'commercial spirit'. However, the German thinkers provided the most systematic reaction in terms of some overall, philosophically based, interpretation of the place of man in society. But by the mid-nineteenth century and since, there has been an explicit British tradition of thought on this subject through William Morris, Thomas Carlyle, Matthew Arnold, John Ruskin, through the Guild socialists such as Orage and Penty and the political pluralists such as Maitland and Figgis and up to our own day with D. H. Lawrence, F. R. Leavis, T. S. Eliot and Raymond Williams. The major point to notice initially about this list is that it is dominated by literary rather than philosophical figures. No doubt there were philosophers, Bradley, Green and Bosanquet, who were committed to the communitarian ideal but their thought had not perhaps the contemporary influence or the succeeding influence of these other figures. Secondly, a mere inspection of the above list underlines the point made in the context of the continental theorists discussed in the previous section, namely that even though these thinkers may be regarded as committed to the communitarian ideal, the nature of their commitment is very far from being unidimensional. What they take to be central to the idea of community varies with their overall standpoint. T. S. Eliot, who had so perceptively diagnosed the loss of community and attachment in *The Waste Land*, linked his idea of community with his overall Christian commitment. In *The Idea of a Christian Society* (1939) and *For Lancelot Andrewes* (1928) he formulates these ideas in some detail. He rejected the idea of a society which had no stronger beliefs than 'a belief in compound interest and the maintenance of dividends' and saw a truly communitarian society based upon shared beliefs mediated by the established Anglican church. As the title of his earlier essay on Lancelot Andrewes suggests, the inspirational source for Eliot's views appears to have been Elizabethan society and in particular its ecclesiastical settlement. The other major literary social critic of the period, F. R. Leavis, approached the problem from a different range of values and in consequence what he stresses in the notion of community correspondingly differs. Indeed, in terms of the thinkers discussed in this essay, Leavis seems to have much in common with the Tönnies view of community. For Leavis community refers primarily to the complex set of values relating to organic rural society. The industrial revolution had fractured this form of communal experience and, as he says in an issue of *Scrutiny* in the 1930s, we are at present witnessing a 'breach of continuity and the uprooting of life, of immemorial ways of life rooted in the soil.' It was with Denys Thompson in 1933 in *Culture and Environment* that this way of looking at present day society against the yardstick of the rural community received at Leavis's hand its most concrete articulation (1933, p. 87):

> The old England was the England of the organic community
> and in what sense it was more primitive than the England that
> has replaced it needs pondering. But at the moment what we
> have to recognise is that the organic community has gone....
> Its destruction in the west is the most important fact of recent
> history.

This tradition of talking about community in such a way as to restate the values of the old rural ethos has a history which goes back to Goldsmith, Crabbe and Sturt. Whereas the German communitarians tended to look a long way back to the Greek polis for their image of community, British communitarians have more often than not looked back to the village community which was beginning to be destroyed in the second half of the eighteenth century, if they did not go further with William Morris and see in feudal society the appropriate image of community. The logic involved in looking outside of one's own social context for a revised picture of human nature and the forms of communal life will be discussed later in this essay but it will then be argued that this kind of activity is endemic in radical social criticism.

Both Eliot and Leavis are conservatives, trying to restate different values from a different age and rejecting central features of modern urban industrial society. But there are others within the British tradition who look to the notion of community for a radical answer to present social problems and discontents. Prominent here is Raymond Williams (1961 and 1965) who has tried to defend a view of community in terms of co-operation, fraternity, participation, egalitarianism and a sense of membership. Whereas Eliot and Leavis are both in their different ways élitists, Raymond Williams's attempt to make coherent the idea of a common culture is egalitarian and much influenced by the views of Marx.

Again, as can be seen within the British tradition of thinking about community, what is taken to be central to the descriptive meaning of community trades upon the general ideological position of those operating with the notion. So to suggest, as Bell and Newby implicitly do and as Hillery certainly does, that it is possible to formulate some scientific, non-contested descriptive meaning of community betrays a misunderstanding of the logic of the situation and an insensitivity to the extent to which the historical career of a concept structures our present understanding of it.

Possibly within the context of British theorising about community the most famous and certainly the most often quoted passage is from Disraeli's *Sybil* in which the foregoing point about the relationship between evaluative and descriptive meaning is borne out in a specific case. The following conversation takes place, significantly enough, in the ruins of a medieval monastery (Penguin edition, 1954, p. 40):

'As for community', said a voice which proceeded neither from Egremont nor the stranger, 'with the monasteries expired the only type we have ever had of such intercourse. There is no community in England: there is aggregation but aggregation which make it rather a disassociating principle rather than a uniting principle...Christianity teaches us to love our neighbour, modern society acknowledges no neighbour.'

In this context the notion of community is being implicitly defined in a conservative way in terms of a way of life which has been *lost*, and which is further seen as being incompatible with the central ethos of modern society with its differentiation of function and anonymous form of social interaction. Given this kind of view of community, it would be necessary to say that community work is either a misnomer for a particular form of social work or that it is a definition of an impossible kind of enterprise. In so far as the community worker's aim is at least in part to foster the development of community within modern urban industrial society he has to take part in this debate about the meaning of community which, as has been argued, is not about 'facts perceived through the senses' in Hillery's phrase, but is rather a debate fundamentally about the kind of society in which we *ought* to live.

Certainly within community work theory many elements of the analysis in this chapter are to be found. Many of the same factors are there to be found in the formulation of the ideal of community—industrialisation, urbanisation, the development of large scale bureaucracies and the increasing complexity of all sorts of social organisation. As an article in the *Journal of Community Development* put the point (Hendriks 1972, p. 76):

> The starting point for community development in Western Europe is not as in some other regions of the world to be found in low income subsistence farming areas, but rather on the fringes of a highly organised market economy with great economic and social mobility. In this environment, characterised by industrial development, urbanisation and specialisation, the local community as a living entity was endangered.

The context of community work is thus seen by this writer in no doubt very general terms but terms none the less which have a very considerable overlap with the factors discussed above. This point may perhaps be further reinforced by a *collage* quotation from easily the most influential book on community work and development published to date. In *Community Work and Social Change*, the authors define the context of community work thus (1968, p. 9-10):

> The intensified growth in economic, social and geographical mobility accentuated by the Second World War and its aftermath has created or made manifest new needs in the community field....These may be viewed from three angles: situations whose impact is clarifying the need for community work include the movement of large numbers of people to new towns and housing estates which creates a whole range of community needs and potential tensions which demand action...; the effects of these changes in terms of social change and its consequences for people: these changes mean that because of specialisation, diversity and mobility and because of the physical features of urban living the kind of community life which traditionally was based upon the neighbourhood is rare....This frees people from what they do not like, but it leaves them on their own. Man wants the security which a large scale organisation can afford, but at the same time he craves the ability to shape at least a part of his own destiny. These opposing tensions have not anywhere been reconciled and it is not only the hidden persuaders of the commercial world but also the scale of central and local government, of industry and the social services that limit opportunities for active participation and decision....

> There is also a need in community planning to think in terms
> of whole persons and of the satisfaction of the needs of persons
> in social interaction with others.

In this quotation we are able to identify the features continually
referred to in this chapter: the positive value of community life,
thus endowing the notion of community with evaluative force and
the realisation that this community life is in danger of being lost as
a result of urbanisation and urban renewal, the specialisation of
function, the growth of complex organisations and bureaucracies,
the loss of the notion of the total person in the anonymity of urban
life. In this sense there is no sharp break in the ideology of the
contemporary community worker and those who formed the
sociological tradition which has so structured our thinking about
community life.

Freedom, individualisation and the loss of community

While it is true that the notion of community and its recovery has to
a great extent dominated social thinking over the last 150 years and
that community work may be seen as an extension of this theoretical
concern to practical realities it would be wrong to give the impression
that the sense of loss of the community had only given rise to the
kind of reaction discussed thus far in this chaper. Granted that
there were, as we have seen, different sets of emphases among those
imbued with the communitarian ideal, there were many thinkers
and still are many who have taken the opposite view from the community theorists, namely that the loss of community is *no* loss at all,
in fact it has been a liberating and emancipating development.
Many thinkers, particularly in the seventeenth and eighteenth
centuries, tried to come to terms with the new world—with incipient
market society, industrialisation, specialisation and urbanisation and
attempted to provide an understanding of the nature of man and his
place in the world which would justify the loss of the old com-
munalities. This tradition of thought sought the basis of human
association not in tradition, habit and custom but in the contract
and consent of free persons. The individual, emerging as he was
during this period from the rigid status groups of feudal society
was taken as the basic reality and all forms of social interaction
were to be taken somehow as constructions out of the motives and
desires of these palpable, free, self-conscious individuals who derived
their freedom and consciousness of themselves precisely from the

decline and loss of closer, communal forms of social relationship. The rules of civil society, economic structures and even the family were to be taken as artificial, derived from some presupposed contract between individuals. These artificial bodies were to be taken as creatures of convenience only; man owed nothing to them in that he could come to self-consciousness without them; all that they did was to remove various sorts of inconveniences from private pursuits. This natural law and contract view of human society was an attempt at a systematic level to make sense of social reality in terms of a system of concepts which took the individual as basic. The theorists of this tradition, who have as many individual differences in emphasis as those of the communitarian tradition were mainly Grotius, Hobbes, Hume and Bentham, and they have had as much influence upon our thinking about society as have the community theorists. As Nisbet has pointed out, not surprisingly, such thinkers were not at all sympathetic to the notion of community (1967, p. 48):

> Groups and associations which could not be vindicated in these terms were cast into the lumber room of history. Few traditional communities survived examination by natural law philosophers in the seventeenth and eighteenth centuries. The family was generally accepted of course, though we find Hobbes using a tacit contract type of argument to justify the parent child relationship.... Guild, corporation, monastery, commune, village community, all of these were regarded as being without foundation in natural law. Rational society like rational knowledge must be the very opposite of the traditional.

The loss of community understood in this way was, therefore, a necessary condition of the emancipation of the self conscious, self-directing individual and, as late as the end of the eighteenth century, by which time the reaction in favour of the reformulation of community had set in, Jeremy Bentham, the great utilitarian philosopher attempted to build up a whole social and moral philosophy out of a set of statements about the necessary trajectory of *individual* motivation.

Perhaps though, the best example of this kind of theorising and certainly its most gifted and astringent exponent was Thomas Hobbes and his view of representation may be taken as a paradigm case of the individualists' idea of the unity of human society as being both contrived and artificial. In *Leviathan* Hobbes's starting point is that of the individual and his will, and social solidarity is secured via the legalistic notion of *representation* (1955 edn, p. 107):

> A multitude of men, are made one person when they are by one man, or one person represented; so that it be done with the consent of everyone in that multitude in particular. For it is the unity of the represener, not the unity of the represented that maketh the person one. And it is the represener that beareth the person and but one person; and unity cannot be otherwise understood in multitude.

This way of thinking certainly had very profound effects. Even among those imbued with the communitarian ideal there was a conscious attempt very often to reformulate an understanding of community in the modern world which would take account of the degree of individual freedom which the anticommunitarian thinkers saw as the chief benefit of the decline in the traditional community. The development of individualism has freed men from the constraints of the traditional primary community but there had been losses too. G. B. Parry implicitly points to the ambiguity in the value of the traditional community in a study of Locke's views (1964 p. 164):

> If this order gave the member little scope for independent action and offered little variety of life, it offered instead a degree of protection, established by law and group feeling, it offered the certainties of a fixed and predictable status and of well established communally shared beliefs and it offered a sense of solidarity with the fellow members of one's group.

The constraints of community upon individuals have been removed but what has emerged in the view of the communitarian thinkers discussed in the last section is a *mass* society in which individuals are left alone without being able to draw on the support of primary community groups. The dilemma is, as Younghusband (1968) put it in the quotation cited on p. 29 above—that the decline of the traditional community 'frees people from what they do not like, but it leaves them on their own'. Is there some way of understanding community which will enable the freedom of the individual and the co-operation and fraternity of the community to be meaningfully held together?

Many would argue that there is not and would go on to say that the notion of community, because it is so tied to the Tönnies type of understanding of it, is so outmoded that it would be better jettisoned for ever. Two contemporary thinkers, otherwise widely different, may be taken as representative here. Harvey Cox (1968) discusses a situation which may be of particular interest to community workers. He takes up discussion of the reactions of some ministers who were appalled that their efforts to promote togetherness in high rise apartment blocks had been unsuccessful (p. 57):

> In conducting their survey the pastors were shocked to discover that the recently arrived apartment dwellers, whom they expected to be lonely and desperate for relationships, did not want to meet their neighbours socially and had no interest whatever in church or community groups. At first the ministers deplored what they called a social pathology and a 'hedgehog' psychology. Later however they found that what they had encountered was a sheer survival technique. Resistance against efforts to subject them to neighbourliness and socialisation is a skill which apartment dwellers have to develop if they are to maintain any human relationships at all. It is an essential element in the shape of the secular city.

Harvey Cox maintains that there can be no concept of community which is capable of doing justice to the anonymous nature of secular urban life—a life which is a prerequisite for freedom, independence and autonomy. What the communitarian calls, with prejudice, 'anonymity', Cox would call, with equal prejudice, 'autonomy'; what the communitarian would call 'anomie' or 'normlessness', Cox would call 'freedom'; what the communitarian would condemn as the atomistic nature of contemporary society, Harvey Cox would praise as its independence. Not only within the communitarian position are there contested values, as we saw in the earlier sections of this chapter, but the communitarian position is itself a contested one.

The second representative anti-communitarian thinker is Ralf Dahrendorf (1968). Dahrendorf sees in the German communitarian tradition and in the work of Tönnies in particular, something profoundly reactionary and illiberal. (This of course is a very important issue in that most community workers would regard their activity basically as a radical one.) He describes the communitarian tradition summed up and consummated in Tönnies as a 'barrier on the road to modernity' and as 'historically misleading, sociologically ill-informed and politically illiberal'. Historically he doubts the very existence of the *Gemeinschaft* structure and he comments 'There are always and everywhere those who are able to lay down the law and those others who have had to obey and for this reason there have always been conflicts' (p. 129). *Gemeinschaft* is politically illiberal because, Dahrendorf argues:

> The consistent liberal starts off with the badness or at least the incompatible self interests of men which makes it necessary to invent institutions capable of making these divergent interests useful to all.... He gets impatient with the illusion of a community that robs the individual of this opportunity for decision and reduces him from a free person to a bee tied to a hive.

Here again the communitarian tradition itself which is contested from within, is under attack from the outside. Both Cox and Dahrendorf are basically criticising something like Tönnies's view of community as *Gemeinschaft* and, as was pointed out earlier, Tönnies's view was conservative. But is there an alternative? Is there a liberal theory of community, which will satisfy enough of the descriptive criteria of community to make it worthwhile to call it a 'community' and yet one which can take account of the liberal critique of the traditional *Gemeinschaft* type of community. This is quite a central problem in modern social and political theory and for reasons to be outlined in the next section it is an issue which the community worker has to face.

Dialectic and the traditions

In our thinking about community we are therefore in a profound sense heirs to two traditions of thought which often quite intentionally oppose one another. On the one hand there is the communitarian tradition outlined in the early part of this chapter stressing a range of factors—rootedness, a sense of locality, identity of interests, fraternity and a co-operation and a sense of identity communally mediated; on the other hand there is the individualistic tradition which stresses the individual as the logical *prius* of all forms of social life and seeing at the basis of all social experience contract and not habit, reason and not tradition. There is a danger though, in seeing this latter view as being more realistic, more 'empirical' than the communitarian view because of the tangible, palpable nature of individuals and the intangible, impalpable nature of community. To regard the position in this way would be, though, a piece of persuasive definition which will not stand the test of argument. Reflection reveals that our *concept* of the individual is by no means identical with that of his physical body; rather it is every bit as abstract, as 'conceptual' as that of community and society. Even a philosophical view such as Hobbes's which does equate the individual with his body is a revision of our usual notion of the individual which cannot be regarded in any sense as an empirical truth. We shall indeed see reason in the next chapter in the discussion of authority to reject the individualistic approach to the understanding of the nature of human society. This rejection will, though, be one based upon what might be called conceptual analysis rather than empirical investigation just because at this level of abstraction in talking about the force of the concept of human society empirical investigation is irrelevant.

At the same time, however, to counterpose the two traditions, the individualistic and the communitarian views would be a mistake. It was mentioned in an earlier section dealing with the nature of community) that there were and are within the communitarian tradition many ways of interpreting the descriptive meaning of community. Certainly many conservative theories of community have been attempts to restate the values of a rural way of life which has been lost with the development of industrialism and in doing so such theories are obviously open to the kind of criticisms made by the liberal theorists. At the same time, some thinkers have taken the view that the notion of community can be preserved and that the individualist critique can be absorbed. That is to say the values of autonomy, freedom, independence and self direction insisted upon in liberal theory may all be granted a place and a role within an updated notion of community. Thinkers as diverse as Hegel, Schiller, Marx, Bosanquet, Thomas Green and Raymond Williams have been involved in exactly this kind of enterprise. Minar and Greer have posed the problem succinctly (1969, p. 107): 'Our Problem is to abstract the values of community from the historical patterns that have entered it, then translate those patterns into the structure of an expanding metropolitan world.'

The central problem for community theory posed by the historical discussion of this chapter is therefore some clear formulation of the components of a liberal theory of the community and this may be seen to throw light upon a tension perceived by many community work theorists but which has not so far been illuminated by this historical dimension. Most community work theorists seem to be committed to a liberal theory of the community. Obviously the fact that the community worker is a *community* worker and not some other sort of social worker seems to imply a commitment to the ideal of community but at the same time *qua* social worker he must also have a very deep respect for the value of the individual. (The individualistic dimension of social work principles is discussed in Plant 1970.) This dual commitment comes out very explicitly in Younghusband (1968, p. 78) when the centrality of community to the community worker's concern is insisted upon but in the context of 'the dignity and worth of the individual, freedom to express individuality...the superiority of self-induced change over imposed change' and more generally in the same work (p. 4-5): 'The question for community work is whether organisational structures can be devised and people employed to facilitate citizen participation...in short community work is a means of giving life to local democracy.' At the same time the Seebohm report makes very clear that the notion of community work which they stress is not one of nostalgia for a past type of community life neglecting the gains in individuality which the decline of the rural community has brought to light (1968, p. 147):

> 'Our emphasis upon the importance of the community does not stem from a belief that the small, closely-knit rural community of the past could be reproduced in the urban society of today or in the future. Our interest in the community is not nostalgic in origin.

In fact this statement is followed by paragraph 491 in which a great deal of stress is placed upon citizen participation as a means to the realisation of community life in the modern individualistic urban environment. A final point perhaps to show the link between community work and the problem of the definition of the liberal community is the very title of T. R. Batten's important book on community work practice, *The Non Directive Approach in Group and Community Work*. Again there is the commitment to community with at the same time a commitment to the value of the worth of the individual. Community work therefore shares a central *problematic* with social and political theory generally, namely is there a sense and a definition of community which is relevant to modern autonomous individualistic urban life?

The liberal community and community work

The problem is to replace the individualism of the bourgeois era
not by totalitarianism or the sheer collectivism of the beehive but
by pluralistic communal civilisation grounded upon human rights
and the social aspirations and needs of man.

Jacques Maritain: *Moral Philosophy*

Criteria and community

It was stressed throughout the previous chapter that community
has a wide range of descriptive meaning in much the same way as
'game' has and it was also pointed out that the evaluative position
of the theorist may well determine the aspects of the descriptive
meaning to be emphasised. The problem for social theory and, as
we have seen, a practical problem for the community worker on
which hangs the coherence of his own activity, is that of providing
an understanding of community compatible with a standpoint which
involves the recognition of the values of individuality and autonomy.
The meaning of community is not, *pace* Hillery, given outside any
evaluative framework, rather what we take as central to the meaning
of community is parasitic upon our general moral and social
attitudes. Consequently, in this chapter concerned as it is with the
liberal community, a wide range of possible criteria will be examined
in an attempt to single out the range of criteria consistent with a
liberal evaluative standpoint.

The logical point here about definition is considerably reinforced
by another paper by Richard Hillery, 'Definitions of community:
areas of agreement', published in *Rural Sociology*, 1955. In this
paper Hillery assembled some ninety-four definitions of community,
and his own overall conclusion was as follows:

There is an element however which can be found in all of the
concepts and (if its mention seems obvious) it is specified

merely to facilitate a positive delineation of the degree of heterogeneity: all the definitions deal with people. Beyond this common basis there is no agreement.

The same point could be made about Wittgenstein's example of a game. Games are all played by people but, as has been intimated, the issue is not *just* the rich complexity of the meaning of community or of game. 'Game' is not an evaluative word, or at least not a paradigm case of one, whereas within its sphere, 'community' is. The evaluative framework surrounding the word structures the selection from the range of its descriptive use. In what follows, some of the possible criteria will be examined *to determine which of these are consistent with a liberal theory of the community*. To facilitate analysis a distinction will be drawn between *tangible* and *intangible* criteria.

Tangible criteria (a) geographical area or locality

Certainly historically speaking, locality and geographical area have been important and perhaps central components of the idea of community. This general historical observation is certainly brought out in the case of Germany where, as we have seen, many of our modern preoccupations with the idea of community arose. In Germany there are two words for community—*Gemeinde* and *Gemeinschaft*. The first word refers explicitly to the local community, the second has a meaning beyond it. Not surprisingly, as König remarks in *The Community* (1968), the two usages were originally very closely linked: *Gemeinde* in medieval times referred to the totality of citizens owning equal rights to land and hence locality or place defined community in this sense; *Gemeinschaft* was also used at this time to refer to a piece of land held in common by free men. The position now has changed. *Gemeinde* has retained its original sense, if not its reference, and might now be idiomatically translated as 'neighbourhood'; *Gemeinschaft* though, has a wider sense now referring, as it were, to the *quality* of the relationship of people in a particular place or locality or belonging to a particular group. In English too, we have to distinguish these two senses of 'community', as for example Heraud does in *Sociology and Social Work* (1970, p. 84), in terms of residence community (*Gemeinde*) and moral community (*Gemeinschaft*).

Certainly the word 'community' is often used as a synonym for 'locality' particularly when it stands as an adjective, as in the following cases: community school, community care, community church, community centre. In these cases the prime reference is to a specific locality, or *Gemeinde* but in these cases it seems though, that the *Gemeinschaft* or moral dimension is not entirely absent. It seems evident that when one speaks of community centre or community school, there is some implication that these institutions exist not *just* within a locality, or for a locality but rather to assist the development or the transformation of that locality or *Gemeinde* into a community in the moral or *Gemeinschaft* sense. Certainly the notion of a community school is used in this way in the Seebohm report (p. 155) when it is argued that: 'A community school is one in which the facilities are to be open for use after school hours *to facilitate the social development of the people within the locality*' (italics supplied). A community school or centre is fixed in a locality or a neighbourhood but the implication is that they will, by their facilities, transform the social relationships of the locality into more fraternal co-operative ones. This entails that locality is not now to be taken as a sufficient condition of community as perhaps it once was. The fact that the neighbourhood or locality relations *need* to be transformed by the operation of community schools, centres, etc., presupposes that the moral or *Gemeinschaft* aspect of community cannot be taken as being sufficiently linked with that of locality and neighbourhood. Of course the same point follows after reflection on the *point* of community work. The community worker is certainly perhaps a worker within a particular locality and the word 'community' in the title certainly indicates this, but at the same time, the use of community in the description of the activity goes beyond this: the use of the word implies more than the geographical setting of the work—it refers to the *point* of the work—that the worker is in a specific locality in order to foster and develop some sense of community. A good example of this commitment to some idea of the moral community is given in Batten (1967, p. 15):

People who work together in a group or a project they have all chosen in order to meet some need they all share tend to get to know and to like and respect one another, and to think and talk of themselves more as 'we' than as 'I' and 'they'....It is this change of attitude towards others which *may* result from a project which is at the core of all true community work.

Here, those who work on the project may all belong to the same locality, but the very fact that community work is needed within the locality in an attempt to transform the social relationships in the locality entails that locality is not to be regarded as a sufficient condition for community. Consequently as the philological discussion at the beginning of this section implied, community is no longer an exact synonym for locality. It is a mistake to conclude from the fact that most localities have a well developed sense of community that locality is a sufficient condition for this, for as König argues (1968, pp. 16-17): 'Only too often the outward fact of spatial proximity of a *Gemeinde* is taken without more ado as an indication of an inner integration. But these two things are not necessarily coincident as experience has frequently shown.' Or for that matter as the very existence of community work entails.

If locality is not a sufficient condition of community, or if *Gemeinde* is not a sufficient condition for *Gemeinschaft*, can we say that it is a necessary one? Do all communities have to be rooted in a specific locality even though the mere fact of locality does not entail community? The answer to this question is extremely controversial and, for the first time, reference will have to be made during the discussion to the overall ideological framework which enables these questions to be settled. Many theorists are willing to allow for the existence of *functional* communities. That is to say communities based upon some sense of identity of specific interest which need not imply spatial proximity between those who have the interests in common. Such functional communities trade off the specialised areas of interest generated by the division of labour, a factor which, as we saw in the previous chapter, many of the community theorists considered to be *destructive* of community. Yet here, there are social theorists who argue in terms of community being linked to sectional interests developed by the differentiation of function—the consequence of industrialisation and urbanisation.

It might well be argued by those theorists who are critical of the notion of functional community that the word 'community' in this context retains the evaluative dimension while *totally* altering the descriptive meaning of the word and that this move is illegitimate. The critic might argue that it is rather like trading on the evaluative meaning which the word 'industrious' has and yet using the word to refer to an incompatible set of features. This is not just an academic issue but is one related to community work practice because in the Seebohm report functional communities are given recognition (p. 147): 'The definition of a community, or even a neighbourhood is increasingly difficult as society becomes more mobile *and people belong to communities of common interest,* influenced by their work, education or social activities as well as where they live.' Is a functional definition of community possible or does it use the word while evacuating it of all the descriptive content which it has hitherto possessed? If a coherent justification of functional community can be given, then this would entail that a specific locality is not a *necessary* condition for the reality of community. The answer to this question cannot be given by attending to a group of, as it were, 'brute facts' about the real nature of social reality but by attending to our evaluative position. Certainly what was called in the previous chapter the 'conservative theory' of community would find very great difficulty in conceding recognition to the functional idea. The conservative definition was formulated in some ways as a specific counterpoint to the loss of face to face contact, the growing specialisation, the fragmentation and the mobility of urban-industrial society. In so doing the opposite dimensions were stressed within the idea of community—locality, primary and total forms of personal interaction, shared values in the totality of life, fixed forms of status and role. The conservative may well claim that this is the 'real' meaning of community but, as was pointed out in the context of 'game', this kind of claim neglects the possibility of a wide ranging set of usages. It sanctions *one* range of usage from within *one* particular framework of evaluation. It is then open to a theorist with a different range of values to defend a view of community predicated upon a different range of descriptive criteria. This has been done recently by many sociologists. N. Dennis in his paper 'The popularity of the neighbourhood community idea' in R. E. Pahl's *Reader in Urban Sociology* (1968) has argued in favour of a redefinition of community in the light of the decline in the importance of the locality as a base for social interaction and as a source of social solidarity. Functional community has been defended by Minar and Greer in the following way, and it is perhaps instructive to compare this with Nisbet's rather conservative definition of community cited above, page 31 (1970, p. 140):

Functional specialisation pulls men out of an important part of their interaction with their neighbours and bodies of specialised men themselves become communities but communities independent of place. They develop within themselves the loyalties, sense of identification and other marks of the cohesive sub-culture. Thus the factory, the trades union, the corporation

structure become communities bound together by shared
function rather than by shared space.

Much the same thesis is argued in another significant paper by
Melvin Webber (1962). In 'Towards a reformulation of community
theory' in *Human Organisation* (1957) R. L. Warren has succinctly
discussed what is at stake here, namely some notion of community
which is applicable to the modern metropolitan world and one
which is not bound up with nostalgia for a lost rural ethos, with its
emphasis upon fixity of place and role (p. 66):

> With this progressive fragmentation of function the problem of
> community coherence arises. Can the increasingly specialised
> parts be kept in co-ordination? Can the increasingly specialised
> interest groups work together for community goals?
> If the analysis so far is sound, then the major weakness of
> contemporary community theory becomes apparent. Conven-
> tional community theory is set up to emphasise the horizontal
> axis, the factor of locality, the factor of common interests,
> common life and common associations and common institutions
> *based upon locality*. And it is just this factor which is becoming
> progressively weaker as time goes on.

It is also possible to defend such a view of community on more
abstract grounds too, as being beneficial to those who compose
such functional communities, but also in increasing the sense of
solidarity in society but basically from an individualistic point of
view. The view is an old one and goes back to von Humboldt and
Kant but has been powerfully restated by John Rawls (1972). In this
book Rawls tries to offer a conception of social solidarity which can
also encompass individuality and the loss of the homogeneity of
human experience through the progressive division of labour. Rawls
bases his argument on the point that no one person can do everything
that another person can do, nor everything that he himself might do.
Each person's potentialities are greater than he can hope to realise
and they fall short of the powers among men generally or the human
race taken as a whole. Because of this fact about human beings
each man must select which of his interests and possibilities he wishes
to encourage and in encouraging his own particular interests he will
come into contact with others with whom he will co-operate in
realising their common venture. Social solidarity arises not out of
organic unity but is based upon co-operation within discrete spheres

of interest arising out of the division of labour but it soon passes beyond this rather unhopeful beginning for as Rawls argues (p. 523):

> We are led to the notion of the community of humankind the members of which enjoy each others' assets and individuality elicited by free institutions and they recognise the good of each as an element in the complete activity the whole scheme of which is consented to and gives pleasure to all.

So far from functional groups, based upon common interests and aims, being destructive of community so far as they are recognised as complementing one another may well lead to a situation of functional solidarity in which each person within a nexus of particular groups sees in the groups of which he is not a member ways of achieving the human ends, values and potentialities which he has decided to forego. However this may be, the conservative critic of functional community might take the view that to argue as Warren does is merely to restate the problem and not to show that functional community makes sense. To try to show that it does, reference will be made to W. J. Goode's cogent analysis of the criteria of functional community in 'Community within a community—the professions' in the *American Sociological Review* (1957). Goode argues (p. 154) that the professions, albeit functional groups, may still be called communities because of the presence of the following criteria:

(a) The members of the profession are bound together by a sense of common identity arising out of their functional position.

(b) Once a person has joined a profession and thus a functional community he very seldom leaves it.

(c) The members of the profession share values in common, again derived from their functional context.

(d) Within the areas of communal action there is a common language which is only partially understood by outsiders.

(e) The profession has authority over its members and provides rules for activity within the professional sphere.

These seem to be criteria enough for agreeing that the notion of functional community makes sense. Certainly there is no reference to locality and this would entail that locality is not a necessary condition of community but, at the same time, there is reference to other factors which even the conservative community theorist, attached to the locality idea would still accept.

The functional community makes sense and it does cohere with an overall liberal position which, as we have seen, the community work theorist, in common with other social and political theorists, accepts. The liberal position was taken to be one in which the notion of community was to be broadened to encapsulate the values realised by individuals in modern urban society and the framework for this, it was argued in the previous chapter, was precisely the decline in the ties of the local community and the development of specialist functional groups.

The sceptic might still argue that this kind of abstract analysis has very little to do with the actual practice of community work—that community workers will do what they do irrespective of fine theoretical distinctions. However, it is debatable whether this is *just* a fine distinction because it is one which, if accepted, could make a difference to practice. If it is admitted that any attempt to recover the feelings of social solidarity and interaction, so characteristic of the rural community, is bound to be frustrated in the modern world with its moving population and complex organisations, then it seems that if the notion of community is to mean anything at all, it must take into account groups based upon functional interest. Consequently, the community worker in attempting to develop some sense of community, would be best employed in attempting to develop a sense of functional interest. For example, in a housing estate run by a local authority it may be impossible to develop a sense of overall community based upon attachment to place with the shared values which derive from shared experiences and patterns of upbringing, but it could be possible to develop various forms of functional community—one of an overall nature, being for example, based upon the fact that all members of the housing estate are tenants of the local authority. The aim is less to create an old fashioned neighbourhood community but rather complex types of functional communities, some broader based than others, within the area in which the community worker operates.

Tangible criteria (b) the racial community

Racial differences are tangible, detectable differences and, as such, may become part of the criteria of community. A community exists only in so far as it is determinate and has some fixed identity which marks it off from other sorts of social organisation, and racial characteristics, because they are so obvious, may well fill this need to be sure of the identity and limits of community. Certainly to regard race as a component of community accords with common usage.

We talk for example of 'the Jewish community in Manchester' or 'the Asian community in Bradford' or 'The West Indian community in Brixton'—all of these are commonly used expressions and certainly this dimension of the meaning of community is borne out by the examination of the historical sources of the notion. A racial dimension to community is certainly implicit in those views of community such as Tönnies's which stress the intrinsic relationship of community to blood and kinship. The most extreme form of this view, not uninfluenced it may be said by Tönnies's own analysis, is to be found in the intellectual history of Germany in the 1920s. The so-called new conservatives such as Sombart, Spengler, Müller van der Breck formulated the idea of a *Volksgemeinschaft*—the community of the racial people living on the historic, folkish soil of the race. In the slogans of this way of thinking, blood and soil are brought together in an emotive and chilling manner in a view of community which stresses kinship ties, racial ties and the rootedness in a particular locality. To mix the racial people and to be removed from the historic land of the people would therefore be to destroy community. In addition, in stressing such a view of community many of these new conservatives, naturally enough in view of the analysis in Chapter 2, were also very hostile to the cosmopolitan ethos of industrial capitalism (see Plant, in Cox and Dyson, 1972, vol. II.) This way of articulating ties of race and of locality was, no doubt an extremity, but it is still a part of the way in which many think about community as perhaps the title of the classic study of West Indian immigration in London shows: *Dark Strangers* in some way encapsulates this view of community. In such a strange and racially mixed setting, Bentham's question 'Who are you and with whom do I deal?' which sounds the death knell of traditional community, is a particularly pertinent one.

In dealing with race as a criterion of community, however, two distinct claims have to be kept in mind. One, very extreme claim, is that racial differences *per se* are important—that just the biological fact of different physical characteristics is itself an important source of disruption to a settled communal life. The other, less extreme, form of this claim is that racial differences are *signs* as it were, of cultural and value differences. If community depends upon a shared view of the world, on shared values and interests so it might be said, then racial differences would be important *instrumental* differences pointing to basic differences in world view, values and interests. Many people may quite easily and legitimately hold this view. The other thesis, however, that racial differences *per se* matter depends upon some kind of metaphysical, intuitive notion of blood which I find unintelligible and consequently am quite unable to discuss seriously.

The second point though, that race is a pointer to cultural and value differences presents a formidable obstacle to the theorist who wants to press the claims of some reformed theory of community in a society with a substantial racial minority. It seems clear that what we have called the 'conservative' view of community, which sees the main emphasis of the descriptive meaning of community to be in terms of locality and cultural and kinship ties, will be unable to make sense of a multi-racial form of community when 'multi-racial' implies that not *all* values are shared and not *all* ends are recognised and this is why, with perfect if manic consistency, the new conservatives formulated the *Volksgemeinschaft* idea. It is not so clear, however, that a notion of community argued in the previous section based upon function rather than locality and overall agreement in values, would have the same sorts of consequences. To share a set of functional interests based perhaps upon one's job or upon one's housing or even leisure interests does not entail that values have to be shared overall. It does seem possible that this liberal functional community will be compatible with a degree of cultural mixing which would not be the case with the conservative view. Obviously it will still be necessary for people in functional groups to take the same view of their interests, and problems about language and value differences will have an effect here, but at least the problem is a more restricted one than trying to generate some overall sense of community in the shared-values-locality sense.

Again this is a point arrived at through analysis, but which may well have practical consequences, particularly in racially mixed societies such as the USA and Great Britain. Community workers are often called upon to be community development officers or community relations officers in racially mixed contexts and if community is taken in Tönnies's sense as culturally and morally homogeneous, then the community development officer can only be engaged on community building in so far as he is involved in trying to make those from the minority group come to accept the overall values of the majority—to encourage all that is covered in a short-hand way by the notion of 'integration'. On the other hand, if a functional view of community is taken, then this need not be so, it will rather be an attempt to develop a harmony of identification of functional interests either based upon the analysis of one's labouring situation, one's housing context or even, from the point of view of those who are consumers of the social services. A community project undertaken *within* a neighbourhood need not then be taken as a foundation for an attempt to generate the old overall neighbourhood ideal—the cultural differences in terms of upbringing, moral priorities, as well as the long-recognised problems involved in the dislocation of work and residence will all militate against the possibility of this ideal being realised; rather what is being attempted is a harmonisation of functional interests within a specific area of life. Of course, this could lead, over a long period, to some wider agreement and harmonisation of points of view because interests, connected as they are with wants and desires, are not detachable parts of a man's personality, but are shot through with his overall value position. But even then, these more total integrations will be based upon identities of functional interests and not upon some mystique of kinship, locality, blood and the rarified capacity for moral empathy.

Locality and race have now been considered and rejected as necessary and sufficient criteria of the liberal theory of community, whereas the notion of functional or interest communities has been moved to a more central position. The major point to be insisted upon though, is that the question of the meaning of community is not to be settled by an inspection of the 'facts through the senses' but by a following through of the consequences of a particular range of evaluations. The notion of the functional community does not refer to some kind of 'brute fact' but is rather an attempt to make sense of the idea of community from some overall liberal view of man, taking into account the values of autonomy and freedom realised as a result of the decline of the traditional community. In addition, it should be pointed out that this liberal view of the community is not some recent invention but goes to the very start of sociological thought on the nature of community because it is arguable that Hegel in his *Grundlinien der Philosophie des Rechts* formulated a theory of functional community based upon sectional interests revealed in the division of labour so central to the structure of civil society (see Plant, *Hegel*, 1973, Ch. VII).

Intangible criteria of community

Community is often defined in much the same way as God was in medieval Jewish theology—that is to say by the *via negativa*, that is, saying what God is *not* rather than describing his positive attributes. This kind of device is often used in community theory—community is *not* society, is not compatible with radical differences in world view, is not compatible with fundamental disagreements over interests, and in the following argument, it must be confessed, the present author adopts much the same rather evasive and tentative procedure.

We are often able to distinguish between two entities, states of affairs or activities by seeing whether or not we are forced to say different things about them and to ask basically different questions relative to each. This is quite a useful procedure at this juncture because it is possible, I think, to elucidate some of the less palpable criteria of community by discussing the kind of way in which we should naturally describe the relationship between an individual and a community, that is in contrast with other kinds of individual-collectivity relationship. In order to facilitate this analysis reference will be made to some distinctions drawn by Raymond Williams in his book *The Long Revolution* (1965), in particular in his chapter on 'Individuals and Society'. Here Williams concentrates on various possible descriptions of an individual's relationship to his social group and it turns out that only one of these descriptions is relevant to man's relationship to a community, and when this particular description is given some precise 'cash value' it specifies, in some broad detail, the structure of community as opposed to other sorts of social grouping.

A person, Williams argues, may find himself in the position of a *subject* or a *servant* in his relationship to his collectivity, that is the individual may find society as a system of repression; he is oppressed by it, he is not integrated into its values which seem to control his behaviour and yet he conforms because he is unable to maintain himself outside of it. Clearly one cannot say in the context of a *community* that a man is either a 'subject' or a 'servant'. It is just not permissible to talk in this kind of way about a man's relationship to a community although, of course, it may be a perfectly intelligible description of his relationship to some other sort of social grouping or collectivity.

Alternatively a person may feel that his relationship to his wider social group is that of an *exile*, that is to say he may be in the position of finding the forms of social interaction and intercourse within the collectivity so deeply alien and completely meaningless that he leaves the group or collectivity. Again this is not a possible way of understanding or describing a relationship to community—alienation and estrangement, the experience of the exile, stands at the exactly opposite pole to that sense of identification and relationship which is so often taken to be the hallmark of both the historical and the functional community.

A less extreme form of dislocation in relationship is that of the *rebel*, the relationship between society and a person who again finds the way of life of his collectivity meaningless but who does not leave it, but rebels against it from within. He does not 'drop out' as the exile does, but he is not able to feel at home in the group because its values are not his. Again this is not, as it stands, a possible description of individual-community relationship. This does not mean that one cannot be critical within a community but criticism is different from rebellion. The critic shares many values and points of view with those whom he criticises and indeed he trades upon such agreements to make his criticism intelligible; the rebel, however, does not seek intelligent criticism and response, but merely rejection.

Finally among possible descriptions of social relationships which are incompatible with talk about community is the case of the *vagrant*, the man who drifts through society but finds its purposes meaningless and its values irrelevant. He has not the conformity of the subject or servant nor the energy of the rebel or exile. Again enough has been said so far to indicate that in this case as with the others one cannot intelligibly talk about vagrancy in the context of relationship to community.

There is, however, a way of describing experience which is compatible with the idea of shared communal experience, that is to say a description in terms of *membership* —the case of the man who finds himself wholly integrated into his social environment and finds in the life of his collectivity something deeply expressive of his own personality, his aspirations and his aims. Only this as yet unanalysed notion of membership can adequately characterise the relationship between the individual and the community or the communities of which he is a member. It is this notion of membership 'one of another' perhaps which the Christian refers to in terms of the complex notion of *koinonia*.

Although the notion of membership has not as yet been analysed, it may be pointed out at this juncture that some such notion, however understood, is presupposed in most discussions in community work theory. It is for example implicit in the Seebohm Report when it comments (Ch. 5, para. 2) that community work must consist in and:

reach far beyond the discovery and the rescue of social
casualties [Williams's vagrants, subjects, and perhaps rebels];
it will enable the greatest possible numbers of individuals to act
reciprocally giving and receiving advice for the well-being of the
community as a whole.

It seems from this that community work is designed to encourage,
develop and enhance feelings of *membership*—perhaps somehow to
change people's description of their social experience from that of
vagrant or *subject* to that of member. Possibly this transforming
element in community work is best brought out in T. R. Batten's
Non-Directive Approach in Group and Community Work) see quotation on page 39). This bears out the point made earlier, that the
community worker links the notion of community with that of
membership, of feeling a part of and identified with a form of social
interaction.

The meaning of 'membership'

Obviously, as it stands, to talk in terms of membership is to talk
about the relationship between the individual and the community at
a very high level of abstraction. It is, only to formally specify the
structure of the relationship and a critic might argue that, even at
this purely formal level, it is not an exhaustive description of the
relationship, and he might here allude to the traditional *Gemeinschaft*
community. Such communities, so the argument might run, could
exist and yet relationships vary very fundamentally between those
who belonged to the communities. Traditional communities could
still exist with very rigid patterns of status and power and yet these
communities are taken by many to be paradigm, even though those
at the bottom of the hierarchy of status would be best classified as
subjects or *servants* rather than *members* of the community. In this
context it would be argued, membership is not the *only* description
of the relationship compatible with the reality of community life.
It must be conceded that this does seem possible, although perhaps
one ought to guard against confusing one's own assessment of a
person's relationship with society with what that person might feel,
as it were, subjectively about his own position. One can only do this
if one has a fairly well-developed theory of *false consciousness* and
yet there are very many difficulties involved in making *that* notion
coherent. (On this see P. Winch, 1958 and 1964.) However, this is
not the basic objection which I have to the criticism. It is that the

criticism is irrelevant in that, as has been stressed continually in this chapter, the community work theorist is concerned with an attempt to formulate a liberal view of community, that is to say one which has assimilated the individualist critique of traditional community and takes seriously both the reality and the consequences of the decline of traditional hierarchies of status which have been eaten away by the development of industrialisation and the acids of individualism consequent thereon. As we have seen the community worker, along with a great many contemporary theorists of community, is as committed to individualism as much as he is to community and only some notion of membership which allows for individual perspective, position, point of view and activity is possible as a description of the relationship between the modern emancipated individual and the communities to which he belongs.

It remains therefore, to give some kind of cash value to this crucial notion of membership, indicating as it does the relation of a modern autonomous man to his community. It will be argued in what follows below that the notion of membership in this modern, individual assimilating context implies both *participation* and *authority* and that in the case of functional community which, as we have argued, is crucial to the understanding of community in the modern world, it also involves the conscious recognition of articulated interests held in common. It may be that the mention of authority in this context may appear paradoxical given that community has been defined in terms of membership, of what Batten calls the 'we' feeling, because does not the notion of authority take us straight back to subject/servant, them and us? In order to resolve this paradox the following section will be concerned to show that the notion of authority is a *necessary* condition of a coherent view of community and not only must a notion of membership take account of this, but also that it is perfectly possible to formulate an account of authority which is able to take account of the individualism so crucial to the coherence of the contemporary view of community.

Authority and community

The analysis of the relationship between community and authority is difficult, but not merely academic. In some cases and contexts the community worker may be called upon to exercise some sort of authority, or to exercise some sort of leadership, so the nature of the authority relevant to community, although a matter for clarifying concepts, is at the same time a practical issue at least for the community worker.

Certainly in the traditional community, the Greek polis, the medieval town, the rural village authority was present but perhaps not recognised as a distinctive and determinable feature of community life. Nisbet in *The Sociological Tradition* (1967) has drawn attention to the crucial but pervasive nature of authority in the traditional community (p. 107):

> In traditional society authority is hardly recognised as having a separate or even distinguishable identity. How could it be? Deeply embedded in social function an inviolable part of the inner order of the family, neighbourhood, parish and guild, ritualised at every turn, authority is closely woven into the fabric of tradition and morality as to be scarcely more noticeable than the air men breathe.

Authority in the *Gemeinschaft* community was thus traditional and customary, a point which is brought out very clearly in the conversation between Antigone and Creon in Sophocles' play *Antigone*. Antigone says of the authority of the laws of Thebes that: 'It is an everlasting law and nobody knows when it was put forth.' Such, however, is not our situation. Social mobility has led to a break in the continuity of man's communal experience and authority and tradition can no longer be linked in this straightforward fashion. We can intelligibly ask, as Antigone could not, 'What is the authority of tradition?' and if we *can* ask this, then it might well appear that whatever authority is left to tradition is accredited to tradition from something *outside* of itself. It we do link community with authority and if we seek a definition of community which is relevant to the modern urban, mobile world, we seem then to be committed to redefining the nature of authority.

But it is just at this juncture that the radical critic might break into the argument with the view that, in fact, authority is incompatible with the modern community, that is to say, one which does justice to the truth of individualism. Has not community in the modern world been defined as a counterpoint to centralised authority in government, in economic and social life generally and indeed in the administration of social welfare? So what has authority to do with community? Indeed the practical emphasis upon a great deal of community action of the radical sort seems to be upon the *un-*

structured nature of such activity and, even in the 'establishment' as it were there is still a strong sense of this. For example in Younghusband (1968) the authors seem to agree with the emphasis just noted, namely that community work is at the opposite pole to organisation and is committed to the values of individualism: 'Part of the whole dilemma is how to reconcile "the revolution in human dissent" with the large-scale organisations and economic and social planning which seems to be inseparably interwoven with the parallel revolution in rising expectations.' In the face of this kind of definition of the context of community work what justification is there for linking community and membership with the idea of authority?

The first part of the justification is general, being concerned with the role of authority in social activities generally, the point being that authority is a necessary condition of any form of social life and thus, *a fortiori*, of community life too. This point of view has been advocated very persuasively by Peter Winch in his paper 'Authority' (1971). The crux of the argument, as it concerns this book, is to be found on pp. 99ff. and because of the importance of this point for what follows later on in the discussion Winch's thesis will be quoted at some length:

The interaction of human beings in society, unlike that of other animals, involves communication, speech and mutual under-standing and, of course, misunderstanding. It is a type of interaction which can be accounted for adequately neither in terms of instinct or conditioned reflex. It follows from this that one cannot give a full account of the nature of human society without giving an account of the way in which concepts enter into the relationships which men have to one another in such a society. Wittgenstein has shown how notions like communication and understanding presuppose the notion of following a rule.... The acceptance of authority is not just something which, as a matter of fact you cannot get along without if you want to participate in rule governed activities; rather to participate in rule governed activities *is* in a certain way to accept authority. For to participate in such an activity is to accept that there is a right and a wrong way of doing things and the decision of what is right and wrong in a particular case can never depend completely on one's own caprice. For instance *pace* Humpty Dumpty I cannot (at least in general) make words mean what I want them to mean: I can use them meaningfully only if other people can come to understand how I am using them.

This is an argument of quite crucial importance. To have a determinate and recognisable form of social interaction involves having shared conventions and rules governing the descriptions which identify and pick out such shared interactions. Actions do not appear as 'brute facts' and they are only shared interactions in so far as they are described by people within the community in the *same* way and what constitutes the same way will be given by the conventions surrounding the description, the rules for its correct use. Any form of human interaction because it is inter*action* and not just reflex behaviour must embody concepts which presuppose rules and these rules are intrinsically linked with the idea of authority.

Such an argument enables us to make two preliminary points about authority and its role in community. A community, whatever else it may be, is a sphere of human interaction and this enables the above argument to gain a purchase on the notion of community. Community, as a sphere of interaction, must be rule governed and thus authority is a necessary condition of community. The second point to be made is that in the case of the liberal community, in which the notion of membership is the operative way of describing the relationship of the individual to the community, this implies that there is some common and agreed view of the process of interaction or some agreed identification of interests and therefore some notion of authority giving point and backing to the use of the concepts to refer to the same thing.

However, beyond establishing that community membership and authority are linked, this argument does not take us much beyond purely formal analysis. Exactly how, in a particular case, authority enters into community will depend, as much else in this book, on how one sees the descriptive meaning of community. On the traditional view of the community, there must be shared concepts overall, concepts relating particularly to morality, to religion and to the description and mediation of social reality. On such a view it is very easy to see where the notion of authority in fact enters the community—it comes *pari passu* with the rules regulating the general and overall descriptions of experience by which the community is pervaded and which in fact form the basis of its communal life.

Such a view of the source of rules and thus of authority is not, however, applicable to the case of the functional community precisely because a functional community is not defined in terms of some *all in all* agreement over values and world views but rather in terms of a sense of belonging to a *specific* group in terms of recognising interests shared with members of those groups. In this kind of context the notion of authority enters not in some kind of *total* fashion as it did in the traditional community, but rather through the notion of role or function which obviously is crucial to the definition of functional community. A functional community is one predicated upon some shared interests resulting from some specialism generated from the division of labour. To talk of a role is to talk in a shorthand way about a shared pattern of activity of behaviour and action. The role of a teacher, policeman and consumer of social services are all oblique ways of talking about regular and determinate patterns of action and these patterns of action have *norms and expectations built into them.* The rules which once merely described the behaviour, which were once extrapolated from the on-going behaviour come to have a normative import, they imply how the activity *ought* to be carried on. It is these rules attached to social roles, which have this normative force which constitutes the source of authority in the functional community. The difference between the authority of the traditional community and the functional community is that whereas the authority of the former was unitary and pervasive, governing the *whole* way of life of the society, in a functional community the rules have authority no doubt, but the functional community is only a particular type of social grouping within a larger social context and thus the authority of the rules overall is not unitary. In addition, the traditional community was pervasive in the sense that it covered the whole of a man's activity and therefore his possibility for consent to the authority was negligible. A functional community, however, does not require this sense of overall commitment. A man may, on the whole, *choose* to join a functional community or not to do so just because its sphere of influence and activity is so much more restricted. In this sense therefore, we can do justice to the central and ubiquitous role which authority plays in social life generally and thus in community while, at the same time, preserving a liberal view of the person. To define community functionally is to recognise a plurality of communities, thus a plurality of roles and functions, hence a wide range of rules and authorities. This pluralism enables us to make sense of social criticism in that one set of rules drawn from one functional context may be used for the criticism of another. This would not be possible with the unitary authority of the traditional closed community.

Although the above analysis is abstract and philosophical this attempt to clarify the relationship between the liberal community and authority has several practical consequences which may be of importance to community work practice. Community is based upon interaction—whether total in the context of the traditional community or discrete and partial as is the case with the functional communities, and it is important to bear in mind that the notion of social interaction involves intrinsically the notion of a shared conceptual framework—again total in the traditional community and partial, relative to the identification of a particular group of interests in the functional community, and that these shared concepts must be used according to rules or conventions. Community, communication and authority thus go together and it is precisely at the intersection of these three that the problems may well arise. The community worker may well be expected to exercise authority, or at least leadership, within the groups with whom he works whether they be locality or functional groups or both, and authority, as I have tried to argue, enters into community through the notion of communication or of shared concepts. Consequently an exercise of authority or leadership to be effective must be *intelligible*, that is to say must be meaningful from *within* the shared framework of concepts of the locality or the functional group. It is precisely at this point that problems may arise because of possible cultural differences between the community worker and the groups with whom he works. This is a point made particularly well in Younghusband (1968):

> Individuals are not born into the total culture of any society, but into a matrix of subcultures which reflect the community, class and ethnic position which the family occupies in the social structure. These subcultures carry with them systems of values which the child learns through the agency of the family and other social institutions.
>
> The diversity of values in society has important implications for community work. It means that the community worker must recognise that he is himself the product of a particular subculture which may have a value system at variance with that community in which he is doing his professional work.

This important point is one which pervades all social work as may be seen in the context of social casework in Timms and Mayer's 'Clash in perspective between worker and client' in *Social Casework* (vol. XXXVI, no. 1, 1969) and the same authors' *The Client Speaks: Working Class Impressions of Casework* (1970). It is very important to realise though, that this issue is not just that of a communications gap, important though this may be, but it is rather more a question of the authority of the social worker. His authority within the community whether local or functional will depend upon his capacity to articulate the aims, needs, wants and desires of the community in terms of the concepts internal to the community which, as we have seen, are definitive of the local or functional community as a system of inter*action*.

This seems to imply on the part of the social worker a necessarily non-directive approach. A directive approach in community work might give a greater impression of the community worker's authority, namely that he knows best, but it will, at the very same time, undermine the authority of the action in that *qua* directive, it might well be unintelligible unless it is internally linked with the system of communication and rules which is definitive of the particular community. In the non-directive approach, however, the community worker has to encourage the community or group within which he works to articulate its own wants, needs and aims.

A final point remains to be made about the role of authority in the community. If communities are defined in terms of either overall or at least partial systems of interaction along with the possession of the attendant concepts for defining and picking out such systems of interaction, and if these concepts presuppose the existence of rules for their use, then it follows that community is in one sense a set of rules. This statement of identity may appear somewhat recondite but an appreciation of it will lead to an avoidance of metaphysical extravagance when talking about community. Communities are often taken in a metaphysical sense and are credited with a life, history, spirit and ethos all of their own. If we concentrate upon the rule-governed nature of community life we shall avoid this tendency which may have and certainly has in the past had wholly unfortunate consequences in theorising about community. (See Plant in Cox and Dyson, vol. II, pp. 73 ff.)

A liberal view of the community cannot therefore dispense with the idea of authority. However much the language of community work may talk in terms of unstructured situations, groups and communities this cannot, if these situations and groups and communities are to be determinate things at all, mean that such groups are without rules and thus without authority. The best way of interpreting such language is perhaps in terms of a not very precise protest against the complexity of authority and the distance between people and their rule-governed contexts ther rathan in terms of a rejection of rules and authority in itself.

Participation and community

> Community development aims at increased and better
> participation of the people in community affairs.
> Social Progress through Community Development (U.N., 1955)

If the liberal community is to be defined in terms of membership, as opposed to subject or servant, vagrant or exile, then it seems that some possibility of participation in community life is required in order for that community to be a community in the liberal sense which we have been trying to define and which is presupposed by community work. Membership involves the idea of identification which seems to presuppose some kind of involvement. Indeed the empirical evidence seems again to underline a conceptual point. Since the very beginning of the contemporary community work tradition with the Cincinnati social experiment in the early years of this century most community workers have seen a very close tie-up between community and democracy understood in terms of some active involvement. With the decline of the older neighbourhood community a good deal of attention has been paid to ways and means of making democratic various sorts of functional groups, whether it be in the sphere of labour, leisure or welfare. Raymond Williams in *The Long Revolution* has noted this development in the case of work (p. 342):

> In spite of limited experiments in joint consultation the ordinary decision-making process is rooted in an exceptionally rigid and finely-scaled hierarchy to which the only possible ordinary response of the vast majority of us who are in no position to share in decisions are apathy, the making of respectful representations or revolt.

Without this fundamental change, there can be no functional community of labour.

Similarly he defines the situation with reference to a housing estate which, if the people are regarded as tenants of the local council, may be regarded equally as a functional community or a neighbourhood one: 'Why should the management of a housing estate not be vested in a joint committee of representatives of the elected authority and elected representatives of the people who live on it?' This linking of community, membership and participation also comes out very clearly in the Seebohm Report, particularly in the chapter on Community in which the Report concerns itself particularly with citizen participation, developing an idea of community based upon membership, of a sense of 'we' rather than 'I' or 'they'. This general point about the Report is particularly true of paragraph 492, an argument which is also echoed in Younghusband (1968, p. 79):

A democratic society exists to enable all of its citizens to develop the various talents and interests to the fullest possible extent. The concern is with the whole man and his ultimate value by virtue of his humanity. . . . it is from participating and sharing in social, economic, occupational, political and religious activity that individuals gain their friendships, find their identity and are able to give as well as to take from the society.

The same argument is made explicit in 'Community Development in Western Europe' published in the *Community Development Journal*, but first published under United Nations auspices (Hendriks, 1972, p. 76):

The individual citizen has ceased to have any sense of his being personally involved: he no longer feels that he is able to identify himself with any organised body. . . . The main question then is how to promote greater flexibility in large scale institutions and to increase their systematic contact with the population or, to put it differently how to transform formal democracy so that it becomes a living democracy. Conscious participation of the population in the development of their own community and readiness to share responsibility are essential if that transformation is to take place.

These are clear commitments to the liberal idea of the community. Indeed the modern ideals of democracy were often argued by individualist philosophers, such as Locke and Bentham, against the rigidity and hierarchy often present in the traditional community.

Community, membership, participation go hand in hand and the development of the theory of community work bears out the formal philosophical analysis which first led us to link these three concepts.

However, it is useful in examining community work theory to look at the particular justifications of participation and broadly these fall into two kinds. There is the argument in terms of efficiency and in terms of the realisation of the nature of man. One a very pragmatic kind of justification; the other a very metaphysical one.

Participation and efficiency

The argument in terms of efficiency is crudely that people who actually belong to the groups know their own needs best. Consequently the community worker in trying to make articulate these needs from within the groups which he serves is serving both the cause of community development by encouraging people to come forward and actively say what they need and thus efficient administration. Those who are concerned with servicing the various functional groups in society, whether they be welfare and housing departments of local government or central government policy-makers, are less likely to make mistakes about the real needs of people if these needs are actively represented to these servicing authorities by the groups concerned. The job of the community worker is then seen as facilitating the articulation of these needs and perhaps helping their presentation to the appropriate body. As is made clear in the Seebohm Report, participation 'relates to the identification of need, the exposure of defects in the system and the mobilisation of new resources.' Much the same point is made in Hendriks (1972): 'The intricate patterns of these relationships in urban areas have not been adequately investigated. Consequently social needs are not taken into account'. How this works out in practice is rather a matter of dispute. The identification of need through citizen participation was a central part of President L. B. Johnson's poverty programme as was revealed very clearly in his message to Congress on 16 March 1964:

> This program asks men and women throughout the country to prepare long range plans for the attack on poverty in their own local communities. They are not plans prepared in Washington and imposed upon hundreds of different situations. They are based upon the fact that local citizens understand their own problems and know how to deal with them.

However, the exact consequences of the programme are still controversial. Ben Whitaker in his Fabian tract *Participation and Poverty* (1968) saw in the measure something of a 'controlled revolution' in an attempt to pass some measure of power over the planning and control of welfare resources to those groups which were to receive them. On the other hand D. P. Moynihan, not altogether without a political axe to grind as he later became an adviser on welfare to President Nixon, described the programme as involving *Maximum Feasible Misunderstanding*, the title of his book (1969) on the subject. (The title is a pun in that the Act of Congress specified that the programme was to involve maximum feasible participation of those involved.)

Pragmatic justifications of what are essentially moral and political ideals always involve this kind of difficulty. It is very often difficult even to know what the criteria of efficiency or success presupposed in such justifications are supposed to be and when the notion of success is so elusive and when the evidence, as the controversy over the US example makes clear, can be interpreted in a very wide variety of ways a moral justification is the only appropriate kind. If such a view of participation happens to maximise efficiency this is an incidental gain, but, as we shall see, a good many of the theorists who would justify participation on moral grounds are often prepared to admit that participation may well lead to a *decline* in efficiency. If what is at stake is community building it is a fundamental error to fudge the issue of participation into one not of what is involved in the notion of community or membership but into one of what maximises administrative efficiency. (There is a parallel problem about the justification of casework principles on pragmatic grounds.) (See Plant, 1970, pp. 18-19.)

Participation, community and self-realisation

The other major justification is in terms of some notion of human self realisation or self fulfilment. To put the point in a rather homiletic fashion quoting from 'Community action: The great need' by R. W. Poston (1953, p. 7):

> Democracy is spiritual in nature. It cannot be measured in terms of efficiency. It is a basic process, a method of communicating, of exchanging thoughts, ideas, joys, sorrows and human feelings. It is freedom to live, choose and be responsible.

The same kind of point is to be found in Batten (1967) and Lees (1972) and more in passing in the Seebohm Report and in Young-husband (1968). These last two are less clear-cut. They do talk of democracy and community building through participation but all the way through both reports there is a tendency to pass over to the argument about the efficient identification of social needs through participation of those with the needs in the policy making of the social services. Batten on the other hand justifies participation in terms of its intrinsic relationship to building a community and in terms of the self-realisation of those within the community (1967, p. 15):

> Most agencies have as their primary aim the development of people in the sense that they want to help them both individually and in groups to develop the will and the confidence to manage their own affairs. They value this not only because it enables people to meet more of their own needs for themselves but also in so doing they can increase their own status and self respect.

It was argued in the previous section that the evidence in favour of the pragmatic justification of participation in terms of efficiency is contestable but in the present case, a justification in terms of self-realisation, there seems on the face of it to be more evidence to go on. Often cited psychological studies in this context, designed to show that in some sense participation does justice to the satisfaction of a wide range of human needs are K. Lewin, R. Leppitt, R. White, 'Patterns of aggressive behaviour in experimentally created social climates', in the *Journal of Social Psychology*, 1939, Erich Fromm, *The Sane Society* (1963) and *The Fear of Freedom* (1960) and H. Maslow's contribution to Kornhauser's collection *Problems of Power* (1957) 'Power relationships and patterns of personal develop-ment'. All of these studies are, in some way, held to provide empirical backing to the idea that participation in some way or other satisfies deep human needs and desires. At this juncture the argument will not be further analysed because it constitutes, by and large, the subject matter of the next chapter. Perhaps the conclusion of that chapter may, however, be presented here, namely that whatever evidence is being adduced in these psychological studies of human needs, it is not in any straightforward sense *empirical* evidence.

Whichever way participation is justified, however, it still remains central to the community workers' position but very rarely in the literature does the argument get beyond this point. The community worker, faced with the task of building, developing and encouraging participation, part of the point of which is to develop communal ties, is very rarely brought by the theorist to a discussion of the social and political context, that is to say to a discussion of what 'cash value' can be given to the notion of participation, however justified, in a modern, complex, highly bureaucratised society. Certainly, we are able to see in community work, particularly in this emphasis on the need for membership and participation a continuation of the ideal of community first articulated in the nineteenth century in which, as we saw in the previous chapter, community was discussed as a counterpoint to an over-organised, over-complex society. But it is at this point that there is the hiatus in community theory. So often participation and membership and the other ideals of a liberal community are left as pious hopes with no effort being made to confront social and political reality, the obdurate and organised nature of which has led to community work, in order to see what are the real possibilities of these hopes being achieved. We should have learned from Hegel and more particularly from Marx's *Der Juden Frage* that changes and tensions in social life cannot be divorced from politics and issues of political power. To be plausible a theory of community, and in particular the place of participation within it, needs to be counterbalanced by a theory of the political organisation of society in which such issues as élitism, pluralism, bureaucracy, democratic theory and organisation theory receive due consideration. Without this the aims of community work, because they *presuppose* but do *not provide* an understanding of the social and political context will always be chimerical. There are wise words on this matter in Heraud's *Sociology and Social Work* (1970), p. 94:

> Thus the attempt to involve people in decisions occurs at a stage too far from the positions where power is actually held and that once more the appeal to the community only results in the avoidance of the real issues, that in commenting upon social situations a means is found whereby attention can be diverted from the social structures.

Heraud is surely correct here and there is an instructive analogy to be drawn on this point with social casework. Caseworkers have often been charged by community workers with neglecting the wider social background of the client—the caseworker, so the argument runs, has concentrated upon a face to face casework relationship in an attempt to 'cure through talk'. Community work has prided itself in going far beyond this to seeing the individual's problem in terms of some more general malaise in his social environment. Community work may, however, be in exactly the same position if the community worker fails to confront by description and analysis the nature of social and political structure in his society and how this relates to his own communitarian and participatory aims. There is a need here to be instructed by the earlier theorists of community, such as Hegel, Marx, Rousseau, Durkheim whose version of the communitarian ideal was always deeply informed and responsive to a detailed and on-going theory of politics and society generally.

Community work and social and political theory

One of the essential components of the community worker's communitarian ideals is that of participation and democratisation, but it cannot be said that as it stands at the moment there has been any really serious attempt on the part of community work theorists to discuss the extent to which this democratisation of functional and local groups can be taken, given social and political constraints actually existing, and the depth to which the political culture of the society at large would be altered if such ideals could be realised. Obviously these are large issues of both political theory and political philosophy which cannot be tackled with any detail here but an attempt will be made to outline the general form of at least some of the issues at stake. The strategy will be to discuss briefly some of the contested theories held about the nature and possibility of democracy to try to see which of these theories seems to have most in common with community work aspirations about the nature of society and politics. Then an attempt will be made to look at both the justifications which can be found for such a theory and the criticisms of which it is susceptible. In a sense then, the point is to try to draw out the political and social theory held by the community work theorist which remains usually inexplicit in his own theorising.

Varieteis of élitism

One of the most obvious and one of the strongest challenges which could be brought to confront the community workers commitment to community development through participation is the understanding of politics and the realities of the possession of political power developed by the élite theorists. The problem of the role of élites in politics and social life generally has been part of the subject matter of political theory on and off since the time of Plato's *Republic* in which the author argued that Philosophers, because they are acquainted with the Good, ought to be Kings. However, the problem has been posed for the modern western world at least by Pareto and Mosca and those such as Michels who have followed the lead which they gave and by the pluralists such as Dahl who share at least *some* of the assumptions of the élitists. Despite differences within the élitist tradition and between the élitists and the pluralists both groups are agreed in seeing very definite limits to the possible participation of the mass of people within political life generally and within significant social institutions and groupings.

The classical élitist theorists, Pareto (1966) and Mosca (1939) argued that political power in society is always possessed by a small homogeneous élite, that the structure of society, at least in terms of the possession of power, is oligarchical. Changes in the élite were to be explained not by the pressure exerted upon politics by the participation of the mass of the people in political life but in terms of there being alternative élites the succession of one by the other being explained, at least by Pareto, in terms of certain irreducible psychological factors operating within the ruling élite as that élite responds to social and economic circumstances. Participatory democracy is an illusion: people always have been and always will be governed, controlled and manipulated by such élites. The psychological factors mentioned above, called by Pareto 'residues' are divided by him into two importantly distinct types, the distinction helping him to explain changes in the possession of political power. Those who possessed class II residues were equivalent to the 'Lions' of Machiavelli—men of honour, integrity, incorruptible, unbending, rejecting government by compromise and dissimulation; those with class I residues correspond to Machiavelli's 'Foxes'—they compromise, are masters of the pragmatic approach to politics, anxious to achieve a consensus, seeing no central role for political principles. All political power in Pareto's view is held by an élite composed of men with one or the other of these general residues or psychological attributes, political change being explained with reference to the interaction between the politicians with the particular residues which characterise them and the context which they confront. For example an élite based on class I residues would be a typically liberal administration operating by compromising between particular interests and attempting to stave off conflict by appeasing those who are aggrieved.

Such a government may well get into a position in which it appears less as pragmatic but more as unprincipled and corrupt. In this kind of context it may well lose confidence in itself and be replaced by an administration with class II residues dedicated to bringing principles and integrity back into public life. The classical real life example of this would be the overthrow of a corrupt government of politicians by an army coup installing generals who wish to extirpate corruption and put national honour and the public interest first. Such a government in its turn, just because it cannot compromise and maintain its integrity, and because it will need class I skills in economic management, may well itself be overthrown eventually by a further class II government. Whatever the mechanics of the process, Pareto is very clear that political authority rests not with the masses, as radical democrats have thought, or with those who possess economic power as Marx believed, but was to be explained in terms of constant psychological factors operating within a psychologically homogeneous élite. How these residues appeared in any culture was variable—Pareto's 'derivations'—but they were to be construed as the correlates of these constant psychological factors.

The pluralists, led principally by Dahl (1961) have responded to the élitist critique of direct democracy, but in such a way that leaves direct democracy without a foothold. What happens in the pluralist thesis is that democracy becomes revised and it is this revisionary notion, not direct democracy which is defended by the pluralists against the attacks of the élitists. The pluralists reject the oligarchic dimension of the élitists' case while at the same time admitting, often only tacitly, the plausibility of the élitists' case against direct democracy. The pluralists see political power not in terms of government by a homogenous élite but rather by the way competing groups are able to present their case to the political authorities which are regarded as responsive to group pressure of this sort. The groups are in principle open to all the citizenry and it is in this dimension that democracy is defended. Direct democracy is ruled out but democracy is revised in terms of this group theory in which open groups press interests with the political authority. People participate in these secondary groups and exert through the group influence on decision making, but they do not directly participate in the political process.

Many of these groups, it might be thought, are the sort with which the community worker might be concerned. If so, then on the revised theory of democracy which is found in the pluralists' view, the community worker in helping with the creation of active participating groups is involved in the extension of the democratic process. As such the pluralist theory of democracy would provide the cash value for the rather unworked-out commitment to participation and democracy which, as we have seen, is endemic in community work theory with a liberal basis.

However, those social and political theorists who have a commitment to the realisation of the ideal of participation have been deeply suspicious of the pluralists' approach to the revision of democratic theory because in their view the plurality of groups on which the revision depends very often appear themselves to be oligarchical and élitist in structure. Critics of the pluralists such as Kariel and Bachrach may well admit the pluralist critique of Pareto and Mosca who perhaps saw political power in too unified terms, but at the same time, they accuse the pluralists of neglecting the possibly oligarchic and élitist nature of the groups which the pluralists see as the incarnation of democracy. This is a very powerful criticism and one which must concern the community worker since he may very well be involved in some of the sorts of groups which both the pluralists and their critics have in mind.

This thesis that social groupings become oligarchical was developed initially by one of the early classical élitists Robert Michels (1958) who tried to show that even an extreme left wing party theoretically committed to a radical programme of democratisation, such as the SPD in Germany, was not itself democratic in structure and organisation, and to summarise his conclusions he formulated his thesis of the 'iron law of oligarchy'—that all lasting social and political organisations develop oligarchic tendencies. The major reason for this, in Michels's view was the development of specialism and professionalism. The professionals come to have a stake in maintaining the *status quo* because then their professional expertise is operative and this expertise in turn means that the non-professionally engaged mass membership of the group are effectively cut out of the decision-making process. Indeed it is quite possible to apply this analysis to something like the community work profession. Hendriks (1972) stresses that the community worker as a professional with a wider knowledge of the workings of society, and more sinisterly with a knowledge of group psychology, may well be theoretically committed to participation on the part of the members of his community group and yet use his professional expertise to somehow steer the decision-making of the group without even the group being aware of it (cf. Lees, 1972, p. 68). Indeed, there is some empirical evidence to show that this in fact takes place. The argument is to be found in Verba (1961) *Small Groups and Political Behaviour* and A. Potter *Organised Groups in British National Politics* (1962). In this latter study Potter divided interest groups in society into 'spokesman groups' and 'promotional groups'. Spokesman groups represent established and conventionally recognised interest groups such as trades unions; promotional groups might, however, come much nearer to the cases with which the community worker is engaged, particularly if he works in the sphere of community development and community action because these groups try to promote particular interests which are not necessarily conventionally recognised. In both sorts of groups Potter found a tendency to oligarchy but for different reasons. In spokesman groups there may be some formal democratic structure but because of professionalisation power would effectively be in the hands of just a few officials. Promotional groups, though, may lack formal organisation but will probably still be oligarchical in that those who have the most time to spend promoting the interests and the issues of the group will no doubt lead it. It can be seen that such a view may well pose a real problem for a community development worker committed to a non-directive approach. In 'Participation at Neighbourhood Level' (1972) G. Williams suggests that the development of participation in local activities in working class areas needs the services of a community development officer largely because the prospective participants may not have much leisure time. The professionalisation of the community worker and the lack of time of those within his community pose obvious problems for the development of oligarchy.

Overall then, the existence of small groups within society does not necessarily mean that élitism is undermined, it may just mean that élites are more widely distributed than the classical theorists recognised and furthermore the confidence of those pluralists ranging from the Guild Socialists in the early years of the century to Dahl and others since who relied on small groups and associations to sustain individuals against the centralised power of the state must be seen to be overdone because such groups may very easily themselves become oligarchically governed hierarchies (see Kariel, *The Decline of American Pluralism*, 1967, p. 2).

It seems therefore from a consideration of élite theory that perhaps the community worker is faced with two sets of constraints on the realisation of his ideal of the active community. On the one hand there is the general institutionalisation of élites within the social and political structure generally—a fact noted by critics of democracy such as Pareto and friends of it such as Dahl and the other pluralists. The other kind of constraint may well come from the community worker's own position and training. That he has a certain amount of professional expertise may well frustrate the ideals of group control, participation and membership which he theoretically espouses. The criticism which comes to mind here is whether there is not something odd in the whole idea of community development in so far as this is undertaken by professionals, in that the fact of their professionalism gives them an authority and a power which may well frustrate the development of precisely the ideals which lie at the centre of their thinking.

The radical democracy

Modern political theory is not, however, fully accounted for in this area either by the classical élitists such as Pareto or by the pluralist élitists such as Dahl. The new democrats reject both views. They are pluralists in the sense that they insist on the social and political importance of intermediary groups in society such as those which engage the community workers interests but they go on to argue, as the pluralist élitist does not, that the democratisation of these groups is both possible and desirable. To examine such a view may well illuminate some of the difficulties of élite theory whether in its classical or its pluralist form and, at the same time, be more positively profitable in that it does seem to be the theory of society and politics which appears most consonant with the somewhat *ad hoc* formulations to be found in community work theory. The major theorists of what might be called radical democracy are H. S. Kariel, particularly his *Decline of American Pluralism* and *The Promise of Politics;* P. Bachrach *The Theory of Democratic Elitism* and T. Bottomore *Elites and Society.* Such theorists emphasise the need to democratise and make available for participation the major social and political organisations and institutions. Power will thus be diversified and a sense of belonging and involvement—so central to the ideology of the community worker—will be engendered. The first thing to note here, is how reminiscent this is of the attempt as we saw very early in the sociological tradition to define small group community experience as the counterpoint to complex social, political and economic organisation. But the new democracy goes a bit beyond a pious hope, so what can the community worker learn from it? How do the new democrats react to the challenge to democratisation and participation launched by the élitists?

Elitist theorists have often made use of studies which try to show that the mass of the people are socially and politically apathetic and do not wish to be involved or to participate. Usually these studies are concerned with voting behaviour and a widely quoted one is *Voting* by B. Berelson *et al.* (1954). The conclusion to be drawn is that most people are not imbued with the participating, fraternal ideal; they wish to remain as private individuals and, in Voltaire's phrase, to cultivate their own gardens. Why should people be expected to develop a community consciousness and a sense of civic involvement when they quite clearly do not demand it (otherwise it would not have to be developed professionally) and when they do not make use of the channels for participation which in fact they already possess? This point may perhaps be shown reasonably topically by looking at a quotation from C. A. R. Crosland's Fabian pamphlet *A Social Democratic Britain* (1970) in which he attacks the views of those such as Mr Wedgwood Benn who would like to see the Labour Party more concerned with ensuring participation not just in politics but in all areas of social life (pp. 12-13):

> Experience shows that only a small minority of the population wish to participate in this way. . . . the majority prefer to lead a full family life and to cultivate their gardens and a good thing too. We do not necessarily want a busy bustling society in which everyone is politically active and fussing around in an interfering and responsible manner and herding us all into participating groups. The threat to privacy and freedom would be intolerable.

(Cf. Crosland, *The Future of Socialism*, 2nd edn, 1964, pp. 254-5.)

This case for the diagnosis of general apathy about participation among the majority of people with the emphasis within such a majority on the privatisation of experience is often held to bolster the case for élitism of one sort or another and must certainly bother the community work theorist. However, the reaction of the radical democrats has been to reinterpret the evidence. They do not cast doubt on the findings of the research, but they do tend by and large to reject the consequences which the élitist holds to be entailed by the evidence. They argue that apathy and the privatisation of life are not, as it were, intrinsic features of human nature. On the contrary they argue that it is *because* social and political structures have become so unresponsive to the wishes of ordinary people and become so large and bureaucratic that they cannot become involved that this privatisation of experience has gone ahead. Men have become conditioned to apathy by an over-organised society. The solution is seen not so much in being realistic and accepting the alleged facts about human nature and its under-developed social motivation but rather in developing this side of men's personalities by *making* participatory institutions. It is seen as an educational objective: people have to learn again to be active citizens and it is not too far-fetched to see community workers, particularly community develop-ment workers as being in the vanguard of this movement (see G. Williams, 1972). This response to the apathy argument which is thus of crucial importance not just to political theory but to community work is developed strongly by Bachrach in *The Theory of Democratic Elitism* (1967, pp. 33 ff).

We have noticed in the context of the community worker's justification of participation that one counter argument to the participatory theory is that it is not efficient. Participation is, as we have seen a communal virtue; whereas efficiency is a virtue of organisations and bureaucracies to which communities have often been counterpoised. A clear example of this dilemma between efficiency and participation is provided in a paper on American experience in community development, R. L. Warren's 'Towards a reformulation of community theory' (1957):

> Communities like individuals have a right to self-determination. In community organisation the worker enables the community to develop its own policies, plans and programmes. They are not superimposed....We can hear the harassed public health official or representative from the state mental health depart-ment saying 'If I had to wait for the communities in my district to examine the various needs and decide which ones must have priority and then hope that my programme was included, I would never get anything accomplished.

Obviously the clash between participation and efficiency is a symptom of the wider clash between community and organisation which was intimated above and, as such, it is a basic clash in social values. In *The Decline of American Pluralism* and *The Promise of Politics* Kariel puts this point starkly and relevantly when he says that in advanced western societies it may very well be necessary to choose between on the one hand efficiency, and all that the complex organisation of the modern state has to give, and a sense of self involvement of self development and belonging on the other.

Participation and human nature

Ultimately the difference between the varieties of élite theorists and those who stress both the desirability and the possibility of involvement and participation is a difference in the conception which each side of the divide has of the human person—his capacities and powers. The élitists on the whole have a rather pessimistic view of the human person in which a man's capacities for communal co-operation are regarded as severely limited with élites being regarded as necessary to ensure the stability and coherence of society; the radical democrat and communitarian sees man in far more optimistic terms, as an *intrinsically* social being and not socially inclined merely from convenience or self-interest, craving involvement and deriving from such involvement a sense of belonging and a sense of identity. The former view has its antecedents in Hobbes, the latter in Rousseau, Schiller, Hegel and Marx. Faced with the problems of participation, or with the very existence of community work, we have to make a choice about different and incompatible views of the nature of man and this is one of the most fundamental moral choices which we can make. In a recent article on the growth of community action and of community development 'Power to the people' in *Social Work* (1972) G. Vattano in commenting on the growth of participation and its attendant problems says: 'Some interpret these phenomena as a manifestation of growing anarchy; others view them as signs of evolving more democratic society.' How we see these phenomena and the way in which we evaluate them will be very largely finally determined by our estimation of the fundamental powers and capacities of persons.

4 Human nature, community and the concept of mental health

Consciousness appears differently modified according to the difference of the given object and the gradual specification of consciousness appears as a variation in the characteristics of its objects.

Hegel, *The Philosophy of Mind*

Human needs

In the previous chapter it was argued that the possibilities which we envisage for man's social relationships depend very heavily upon our view of human nature. If we see in man a very small capacity for co-operation we may conclude that the interests of social life demand a large measure of organisation and discipline and a rather smaller measure of participation and involvement; on the other hand, if we take a more generous view of human nature, we may well think that existing social institutions overstress organisation and discipline and should be reorganised to increase participation, involvement and a sense of self-development. But what is involved in the question 'How do we see human nature? Can we derive a commitment to the values enshrined in community work development and organisation, related as it is to this generous view of man, from some kind of scientific examination of the fundamental needs of man? Or does our view of human needs rest upon our evaluative position, so that what are human needs only makes sense within some such evaluative framework and cannot be specified in any way outside it? If the specification of human needs arises only *within* society in terms of its fundamental evaluative positions, then it is difficult to see how a description and specification of human needs can be used as a fundamental critical tool to assess societies.

Needs and human flourishing

We might take as a starting point in the discussion of this complex and important issue a recent controversy in moral philosophy. Some recent moral philosophers, in particular Professor G. E. M. Anscombe in 'Modern moral philosophy' in *Philosophy* (1958), and Mrs Foot in 'Moral Beliefs' (1958) have argued that the notions of human good and harm and of human flourishing, which are so central to moral philosophy, can be derived from and given a content by some description of human needs. As a plant needs water in order to flourish so a man needs the realisation of certain values in order to develop—just because he is the kind of being that he is, because he has the sort of nature that he has. Given that some non-morally engaged description of human needs or *facts* about human nature may be given, then moral values can both be derived and given content.

Certainly this is an attractive argument precisely because it would, if sound, give some kind of base point to moral argument and its attractiveness can also be seen in terms of what preoccupies us in this book, namely do human beings need, in order to flourish, those forms of social relationship which we refer to in rather a shorthand way by the use of the word 'community'? In fact such a move has been made in trying to justify the derivation of the necessity of community by Erich Fromm and Herbert Marcuse, two thinkers who have had a good deal of influence upon the debate over the idea of community in recent years. Fromm in *The Sane Society* (1963) and *The Fear of Freedom* (1960) and Marcuse in *Eros and Civilisation* (1969) are both very explicit in arguing the view that the kind of personal experiences to be derived from communal forms of life fulfils some kind of objective set of human needs, the definition of which is independent of these values and of society at large. Clearly such an argument would possess a great deal of power and would be very useful to the community worker in providing a clear basis for defining, in concrete and definitive terms the shape of the truly human community. A quotation from Fromm (1963, p. 19) may show the relevance of the thesis:

> Sanity and mental health depend upon the satisfaction of those needs and passions which are specifically human and which stem from the conditions of the human situation: the need for relatedness, transcendence, rootedness, the need for a sense of identity and the need for a frame of orientation and devotion. .

.. Man's solution to his own needs is exceedingly complex and it depends on many factors and last but not least on the way society is organised and how this organisation determines the relations within it.

Only those social forms which can in fact satisfy these distinctively human needs provide really adequate frameworks for a fulfilled and adjusted human life. On the basis of his specification of human needs Fromm derives many practical programmes. He advocates radical socialisation, political decentralisation, a reform of education so that instead of being an agent for training people for the anonymous bureaucracies it becomes a factor in co-operative spiritual renewal, and a wholesale return to corporate and co-operative activity and forms of life. Fromm thus tries to delineate the character of the good society from a description of human needs, and given that Fromm's argument is couched in terms of sanity and madness and not good and evil, it seems to imply that his argument has some kind of value-free basis—that his view of man does not itself involve a moral commitment.

This is a crucial problem: whether one can use human nature in this way as a critical tool in terms of which to specify the nature of the good society or community and thus to criticise existing ones, and it is well discussed by Marcuse (1969, p. 203):

Either one defines personality and individuality within the established form of civilisation, in which case self-realisation is for the majority tantamount to successful adjustment. Or one defines them in terms of their transcending content including their socially denied possibilities. . . . in this case self-realisation would imply transgression beyond the established form of civilisation to radically new modes of personality and individuality incompatible with the prevailing ones.

It is thus suggested that even though we live within a particular form of life with its own images and paradigms of human nature we can still transcend these to arrive at, in some sense more objective specifications of the nature of man, his *Gattungsbewusstsein* which, once specified, could become the useful base line for formulating the concrete form of the good society and the true community. This commitment is felt not just by more philosophically interested figures such as Marcuse and Fromm but more substantive figures within psychology such as Maslow who argues (in Kornhauser 1957, p.

107): 'I suspect that psychological health like physical health is in essence universal and that therefore if my impressions are correct all healthy men in any culture will turn out to be democratic in some ways.'

Needs, norms and logic

It might be argued by the critic at this point that even if some specification of human needs could be derived, it would still not function as the critical tool which such theorists want it to do. From the fact that human nature can be given some descriptive specification nothing follows about the desirable structure and shape of the human community. There is a logical gap between statements of fact and conclusions drawn from such facts which contain evaluations. To specify in wholly factual terms the nature of man does not enable us to deduce logically the appropriate sort of society in which human beings are supposed to live. The *locus classicus* of this position is Hume's *Treatise on Human Nature* (1964, p. 469):

> I cannot forbear adding to these reasons an observation which may be found to be of some importance. In every system of morality which I have hitherto met with I have always remarked that the author proceeds for some time in the ordinary ways of reasoning, and establishes the being of a God, or makes observations concerning human affairs; when of a sudden I am surprised to find that instead of the usual copulations of the propositions is and is not, I meet with no proposition which is not connected with an ought or ought not. This change is imperceptible; but is of the last consequence. For as this ought and ought not expresses some new relation and affirmation, it is necessary that it should be observed or explained; and that at the same time some reason should be given for what seems altogether inconceivable, how this new relation can be a deduction from others which are entirely different.

However, irrespective of the merits of this argument generally and how far indeed Hume himself meant it to be taken, it is certainly not fatal in this particular case, because the argument assumes what may plausibly be denied, namely that a statement describing human needs is a wholly factual statement. 'Needs', it might be argued, is a kind of bridge notion. To say that 'X needs Y' is not just to state a fact but it is to imply, *ceteris paribus*, that he ought to get it.

Wanting, needing, desiring, pleasure, happiness and health are all notions which rather bridge the gap between factual statements and normative ones. These concepts can be given a factual content, but at the same time, they usually carry the implication that we approve of their satisfaction (always subject to the *ceteris paribus* clause). Consequently there is nothing in Hume's argument which would, of necessity, invalidate the kind of argument which Fromm, Marcuse and many others have attempted to put forward on the basis of 'facts' about human nature.

Human needs and critical theory

But are there in fact needs which all men share and can these needs be defined and specified in some kind of neutral and value-free way independent of the view of the needs presupposed in a particular social context or ideology? To what sort of expertise should we look for their specification? Since we are concerned with the central powers and capacities of the human mind it might well be thought that it is primarily the psychologist who is in a position to identify these needs in a value-free way.

However, it is arguable that this is not really a plausible suggestion for two closely-connected reasons. Certainly the psychologist will be able to point out certain very formal features of the mind or of human nature: for example that men are capable of rational thought, that they act and are not just acted upon, that they form intentions and act from motives, they have needs, wants and desires. The recognition of these features is valuable and important but merely to list these features takes us a very little way indeed along the road which we wish to travel. In the first place they are formal features of the mind and to claim that all men share them will not take us very far in the argument, because it will not enable us to determine in any detail the structure and the shape of these capacities, and indeed the content of these fundamental needs, to enable us to give some kind of description of the appropriate sort of social experience to satisfy them. In order to do this we should have to go on to say not just that all men everywhere have needs, form intentions, etc., but to go further and show what needs and what sort of intentions all men everywhere form and the motives from which they act. There is no evidence to suggest that this is a plausible or a possible enterprise if it is to be construed as a scientific one. However, the difficulties involved in going to the psychologist for help to tease out the fundamental substantive, as opposed to formal capacities of the mind are even more intractable than this. Even at the formal level in which the mind is considered to be possessed of certain attributes such as wanting and desiring, wishing and willing, there are major disputes within psychology about the meaning of these formal characteristics of the mind. Do they refer to 'inner states' or complex behaviour patterns which require a physiological explanation? One only needs to counterpose Hull's account of so called mental concepts in his *Principles of Behaviour* with the account given for example in *The Concept of Motivation* by R. S. Peters and Charles Taylor's *The Explanation of Behaviour*. The argument is more than a merely academic one because depending upon the view of man which is taken a very great deal turns in terms of substantive issues with reference to human nature and human society. B. F. Skinner's account of behavioural technology (1971) depends entirely upon the consequences following from a rejection of 'inner states' and taking up a more scientific view of human nature (pp. 8-9):

> Although physics soon stopped personifying things.... it continued for a long time as if they had wills, impulses, feelings, purposes and other fragmentary attributes of an unwilling agent.... All this was eventually abandoned to good effect.... yet the behavioural sciences still appeal to comparable inner states.

From a rejection of such 'inner states' wherein are supposed to reside the freedom and the dignity of man, there will be set free a range of techniques of behavioural control and modification which will be based upon a less mystifying concept of a person. The social consequences of these views are well set out in Skinner's own *Walden Two* (1969).

Given the fact that the force of even the formal concepts discussed above are in dispute within psychology and given that the view of the meaning of these concepts is bound to have repercussions on our view of human nature and thus of human interaction, it follows that we cannot look with much confidence to the psychologist to elucidate those features of human life which all men share and which would thus become the basis of a theory of the proper shape of the human community.

Still, it might be argued, this can be done by pointing out that all men belong to the same biological species and thus have certain biological needs in common whatever their cultural differences, and the 'good society' is the one which satisfies these biological needs. Paradigm cases of these sorts of needs would be for example: sex, procreation, the rearing of children, shelter and protection from death and gratuitous physical injury. However, there are several points which can be made about this argument. First of all studies in ethology perhaps undermine our confidence in thinking that there are even shared biological needs of this sort precisely because it is very often difficult to distinguish sharply a biological organism from its environment whether it be a man or a lower animal. However, leaving this point aside, it still has to be said that to specify such biological needs does not take us very far in terms of deriving the appropriate form of human society because most existing societies whatever their internal organisation seem to manage to satisfy *these* needs, indeed it is very difficult to envisage a society which did not and which would still be recognisable as a human society. Fromm implicitly recognises this point because the needs which he talks about which enable him to define the appropriate human society as a communitarian one are altogether different from these biologically specifiable ones. He mentions for example relatedness, transcendence, rootedness and a sense of identity and it is difficult to regard these as biologically specifiable needs. Basil Mitchell (1971) makes this point particularly well when he argues that even at the level of supposed biological needs cultural standards still come in (p. 215):

> Everyone has a biological need for shelter but, when we campaign for Shelter, this is not all that we have in mind. We want reasonable standards of housing and this means *inter alia* some minimum provision for privacy, some access to recreation grounds etc. In tackling the housing problem we aim to provide not just houses but homes where our standards are already culturally determined.

Even at the biological level we cannot escape the relativity of culture.

Above this level, and this is where Fromm's position is argued, it seems that there is now a way of specifying basic human needs outside of a particular socio-cultural context. The content of needs can only be identified within a particular social group or community. Far from deriving society or community from some neutral definition of needs the reverse is the case: what counts as a need, or any other human attribute, capacity or power depends upon the kind of social and ideological context involved. Alasdair MacIntyre has brought this out particularly well (1964, p. 7):

What we desire depends entirely upon what objects of desire
have been presented to us. We learn to want things. Our desires
have a history and not just a biological natural history but a
rational history of intelligible response to what we are offered.

A similar general argument is given by MacIntyre in 'Is a science of
comparative politics possible?' in *Against the Self Images of the Age*
(1972). The predominant influence of the development of this
argument has been Wittgenstein, although it is articulated in the
epigraph from Hegel's *Philosophy of Mind* printed at the head of
this chapter. Instead of seeing a person, as it were approaching the
social world with already determinate and identifiable needs and
desires which demand fulfilment in the social world, the ability to
identify aspects of one's own experience such as a nexus of needs or
desires or wants was taken by Wittgenstein, and those who follow
him here, to *depend* upon a public language, with public rules, set
in a background of social convention, habits and tradition. For
example the identification of an emotion has now been taken to be
intrinsically linked with convention and the public social context to
the extent that what makes a particular feeling a particular emotion
is not the character of the feeling considered as some pure inner
episode or occurrence but the context in which that feeling occurs
and which endows it with the significance that it has (see E. Bedford
Essays (1964)). Similarly the argument would apply to intentions,
motives and above all in the present context to needs. There is thus
a necessary connexion between man and the social forms of life
which he inhabits; far from the nature of society being derived from
some external specification of needs, what counts as a determinate
need will depend upon the way of life of a particular society, and
the particular ideological forms to be found within it.

Even so the critic might argue, there are still certain inescapable
features of human life which are just features of the human condition and are not culturally relative and, philosophical argument
apart, these have to be accepted:

Birth, and copulation and Death.
That's the facts when you come down to brass tacks.

as T. S. Eliot's Sweeny Agonistes says, and this kind of consideration
it might be argued, saves the concept of human nature from total
relativism. (This is Winch's argument in 'Understanding a Primitive

Society', 1964.) However, it will not work and it is difficult to see the relevance of it anyway for the particular issues which preoccupy us at the moment. It will not work because these central features of the human predicament are not just facts or not just, 'brute' facts. Surely these features of the human predicament are always interpreted, assigned a significance and endowed with meaning according to the concepts and conventions of different forms of social life. A good example here is the meaning of 'death'. Death may have a different meaning for the Christian, for the Buddhist, for the secular humanist, for the person tied to a very solid kind of neighbourhood with very close personal contacts and the rootless urbanite with only very anonymous social relationships. These are not just brute facts but are dependent upon the ways of life of societies and particular groups within those societies. In addition even assuming that these were to be considered to be inescapable conditions of human life they would be quite innocent of any logical power to enable us to derive the character of the good society, because if they really are inescapable facts about human nature then of course they are in fact features of any and every society.

Thus it is arguable that there can be no specification of human needs outside of this or that society or form of life. To criticise the way of life of a particular society in terms of some view of human nature, this view of human nature has to be drawn from a context other than the social one which it is to be used to criticise. This is what in fact usually happens. The great German communitarian thinkers drew their inspiration from the Greek polis as did many nineteenth-century Idealist philosophers following the German tradition. William Morris derived his ideals from a romanticised picture of medieval society; Leavis from England before the industrial revolution; Eliot to a large extent from the Elizabethan ecclesiastical settlement and on the continent Maurras from pre-revolutionary France. To do this may be inescapable but it does raise two important questions. The first is obviously the problem of relevance. What relevance has the specification of human needs drawn from a different social system to one's own, particularly when such paradigms of human nature may have been predicated upon entirely different economic and demographic conditions? The other question concerns the status of a judgment about human needs in another context which is used by the social critic. It is clear that it is fundamentally a *moral* judgment rather than an empirical one if for no other reason than that the critic considered the other society with its own images and paradigms of human nature to be *better* than his own.

Ideology and the definition of man

Community and human nature have a descriptive meaning only when they are taken together within a broader framework of evaluation or ideology. From within one particular ideology certain needs requiring certain experiences to satisfy them will be seen as basic: for example relatedness co-operation and transcendence; from, within another framework a less co-operative, less fraternal picture of man may emerge—as we have seen in the disputes between the communitarians and the individualists in the history of political and social thought. There is no way though, of standing outside of these positions in an attempt to settle the issue in some kind of neutral fashion. The concept of human nature and thus of the human community are always and of necessity contested. We occupy a certain position within the development of social institutions and within distinct moral forms, Christian, liberal-humanist, Marxist for example, and the ways in which we come to think of man and his needs and potentialities are from within one or another of these overall points of view. We know therefore that any enquiry into the structure of the human mind and any attempt to connect such an enquiry with the form of an adequate community will always be subject to dispute and will always have to be continually revised. The recognition of this fact, that no one view of human nature has a monopoly of the claim to be the correct one and the tolerance which such a recognition ought to produce is more than one step forward.

This sort of argument renders suspect the point put forward by R. S. Peters in *Ethics and Education* (1966, p. 233) in which he suggests that the differing, contested views of human nature may be reconciled in what might be produced by a co-operative effort on the part of philosophers, psychologists and social scientists. Such an uncharacteristic passion for an Hegelian synthesis on the part of Professor Peters does not really take account of the fundamental ways in which the concept of human nature and thus of community are contested within the various groups in our society.

Choice, ideology and tradition

All of this may (or may not) be granted but what, it might be asked, lies at the bottom of these frameworks of values, these ideologies on which all else seems to depend? The logic of the argument has pushed us back to the point where we must account for the force and the authority of these various ideological frameworks.

The answer to the question lies ultimately in terms of choice. The very existence of competing ideological outlooks and the conceptual conflicts which they engender entails that one has to choose to which one wishes to be morally bound. There is no impersonal standard to which appeal can be made without begging the whole question. We cannot appeal to 'the facts' because in the important cases the very description of the facts is disputed between the ideologies; we cannot appeal to tradition because the Christian, liberal humanist and even the Marxist views may be counted as part of Western European tradition; we cannot appeal to God as an impersonal standpoint because this would be to beg the question in favour of the Christian. Certainly as we have seen only too clearly we cannot appeal to indubitable facts about human nature and the structure of human society. No evaluative framework, no ideology thus forces itself upon us and we are forced to choose between them. The community worker stressing the values of fraternity, participation, membership, communality and individuality commits himself to a range of values of a liberal sort and it is important to realise that they have authority upon him only in so far as he is thus committed to them.

Community and mental health

If we accept the argument thus propounded and reject the idea that the justification of the communitarian ideal can be derived from some precise, value-free description of the human condition then we are also in a position to reject a view very often found in modern writing on the notion of community, namely that adequate community life has something to do with sanity and madness. This view is explicitly stated in the quotation cited earlier (p. 74 above) from Erich Fromm (1963) and it is also implicit in Marcuse's *Negations*. The argument goes like this: sanity involves living in such a way that fundamental needs and drives are not frustrated; when they are frustrated they will lead to mental illness; human needs and drives are such that only some sorts of social organisations are able to satisfy these needs which are concerned with a sense of belonging, rootedness, identity and so on; only a community can satisfy such needs; thus the communitarian society is the sane society. There are intimations of this view in the earlier development of the sociological tradition in particular in Hegel (see Plant, 1973), in Durkheim, particularly his *Suicide* and in Simmel, particularly his *Mental Health and the Metropolis* but of late it has come out particularly in Fromm, Marcuse and Laing and one suspects that there is a good deal of the implicit ideology of this in talk about community mental health and therapeutic communities. To talk about sanity and madness, which are medical terms, however, gives this argument in favour of community experience as against the anonymity of so much of modern life a scientific veneer which is entirely misplaced. If the arguments presented in the previous section are correct then there cannot be any value-free, scientific description of human needs which will enable us to connect community and all that this involves with the notions of sanity and madness. Such theorists may take what I earlier called a generous view of man, but that does not mean that such a view is based upon some neutral examination of so called facts about human nature, for as Alasdair MacIntyre suggests (1967, p. 268):

> I cannot look to human nature as a neutral standard, asking which forms of social and moral life would give to it the most adequate expression. For each form of life carries with it its own picture of human nature. The choice of a form of life and the choice of a view of human nature go together.

The ideological dimension to the meaning of community and the way in which the concept enters into the specification of particular practices and activities is ubiquitous.

5 Postscript: Community work and social casework

It might be useful at this juncture just to indicate briefly what theoretically might be the connexions between the somewhat modish practice of community work and the older but perhaps now more contested and less popular practice of social casework. They may appear to be totally antithetical: community work is concerned with the development, encouragement and maintenance of a particular quality and dimension of social experience, the nature of which has been the subject matter of this essay; casework on the other hand may appear to be more concerned with face to face contact with a particular client with a personal problem. One is rooted in a social and indeed political dimension; the other is a radically individualistic activity, as any examination of casework principles shows (see Plant, 1970). Even so, to regard them in this way as fundamentally opposed is incorrect. In order to show this some reference will have to be made to a crucial argument in Plant (1970). It was argued in that book that in the usual conventional characterisation of the aims of social casework a dual emphasis may be discerned: on the one hand there is certainly the individualistic commitment to the facilitation of the development of the capacities and powers of the individual client but on the other hand there is also stress upon his harmonious integration into his social environment. This point may be seen if attention is paid to the various definitions of social casework quoted in the earlier volume. At the very beginning of the modern casework tradition Mary Richmond (1930, p. 477) writes that social casework is involved with 'those problems which develop the personality through adjustment effected individual by individual between men and society', and in more modern times we can still see this concern with the self-realisation of the individual through his social environment. The famous definition provided by Swithun Bowers may well illustrate this (1950, p. 127): 'Casework is an art in which the knowledge of the science of human relationships and skill in relationship are used to mobilise capacities in the individual and resources in the community appropriate for better adjustment'. Again Corgiat, an Italian theorist, provided a similar perspective (Plant, 1970, p. 52): 'Social service aims to orientate the individual with reference to his own task in daily life and his relationships with members of his family and community.' The aim of casework it thus seems, is by the use of various therapeutic techniques, to help the client to achieve adequate social functioning, to make him an integrated member of his social group or groups, to try to enable the client to participate freely, actively and with self-direction in his social roles and to realise his own capacities and powers within these roles and functions. But isn't this, from a different perspective, precisely the aim of community work, particularly if community is interpreted in a functional way as has been argued in the course of this book as satisfying the criteria of a liberal community? The community worker's aim is to develop and maintain community experience, and this is among other things as we have seen, a sense of integration, free participation and a sense of membership. And it is in much the same terms that the social caseworker sees the solution to the problems in social functioning which beset her clients. No doubt there are differences in emphasis: the community worker stressing the social dimension of individual problems; the caseworker, the individualistic perspective, but it would be a fundamental mistake to regard these as alternative approaches to the pressing and urgent social problems which we all face.

In my earlier book, *Social and Moral Theory in Casework*, I argued for a recognition of the dual perspective in social casework: a commitment both to the individual and to the ideal of community. In this book the same point has been repeated, but the axis of the discussion has been revolved. Instead of discussing the individualistic/community perspective in casework, we have been concerned with the liberal theory of community which involves the same duality of concern and value. John Robinson, writing in the *British Journal of Social Work*, vol. II, no. 4, 1972, of 'The Dual Commitment of Social Work', commented on the practical force of the argument in *Social and Moral Theory in Casework*, and I would like to quote and endorse his views in the context of community work too, to suggest that casework v. community work is a false antithesis (Robinson, 1972, p. 474):

...in any situation the social worker first asks himself, what is the quality of this person's or this family's or this neighbourhood's social experience? Is it possible for people in this situation to feel themselves to be a member of a community? If not, then the work with the environment, of whatever kind, is the first priority. If the problem appears to lie with the individual's perception of society or with his inability to identify with social roles, then casework would be appropriate. In a large number of situations, of course, both forms of activity would be indicated. This way of looking at things explains rather than undermines casework's commitment to the individual. This commitment has arisen not from hostility or indifference to society, but from the feeling that our present society with its increasingly impersonal and dehumanizing features has failed to give the individual the sense of belonging to a community. Casework on this view has been a living reminder of society's need to care for its members and far from being inimical to reform can actually be seen as part of the reforming movement within society.

Suggestions for further reading

In order to tie these suggestions in closely with the points made in the text, recommended books are listed under the relevant chapter.

1 Philosophy and community work

The following books on contemporary philosophy may be useful as introductions to the subject: Cox, C. B. and Dyson, A. E., eds, *The Twentieth Century Mind*, vols I, II, and III, London, Oxford University Press, 1972; especially the essays on 'Philosophy' by D. Bell in vol. I, 'Social Thought' by R. Plant in vol. II and 'Philosophy' by R. Plant in vol. III. Passmore, J., *A Hundred Years of Philosophy*, London, Penguin, 1968; Ayer, A. J., ed., *The Revolution in Philosophy*, London, Macmillan, 1956. At a more particular level the following may be consulted: Plant, R., *Social and Moral Theory in Casework*, London, Routledge & Kegan Paul, 1970; Peters, R. S., *Ethics and Education*, London, Allen & Unwin, 1966; Benn, S. I. and Peters, R. S., *Social Principles and the Democratic State*, London, Allen & Unwin, 1959; Emmett, D., *Rules, Roles and Relationships*, London, Macmillan, 1966; Toulmin, S., *An Examination of the Place of Reason in Ethics*, Cambridge University Press, 1950; Beardsmore, R. W., *Moral Reasoning*, London, Routledge & Kegan Paul, 1969; Mounce, H. O. and Phillips, D. Z., *Moral Practices*, London, Routledge & Kegan Paul, 1970.

The idealists and social work

Richter, M., *The Politics of Conscience: T. H. Green and his Age*, London, Weidenfeld & Nicolson, 1964; Bosanquet, H., *Bernard Bosanquet; a Short Account of his Life*, London, Macmillan, 1924; Hetherington, H. J. W., *The Life and Letters of Sir Henry Jones*, London, Hodder & Stoughton, 1924; Milne, A. J., *The Social Philosophy of English Idealism*, London, Allen & Unwin, 1962; Quinton, A., *Absolute Idealism*, Oxford University Press, 1972.

2 Community as fact and value

The early part of this chapter is very much indebted to the work of Wittgenstein. Discussions of his work are to be found in: Pears, D., *Wittgenstein*, London, Fontana, 1971; Pole, D., *The Later Philosophy of*

Wittgenstein, London, Athlone Press, 1965; Pitcher, G., *The Philosophy of Wittgenstein*, New York, Prentice Hall, 1966. There are discussions of Wittgenstein's importance to social theory in: Pitkin, H. F., *Wittgenstein and Justice*, University of California Press, 1972, and Winch, P., *The Idea of a Social Science and its Relation to Philosophy*, London, Routledge & Kegan Paul, 1958. Winch's development of Wittgenstein's ideas in the field of social theory has been very severely criticised in Gellner, E., *Thought and Change*, London, Weidenfeld & Nicolson, 1965, and Jarvie, I. C., *Concepts and Society*, London, Routledge & Kegan Paul, 1972, and his views are discussed in Wilson, B., ed., *Rationality*, Oxford, Blackwell. 1970. The distinction between descriptive and evaluative meaning is outlined in two works by R. Hare, *The Language of Morals*, London, Oxford University Press, 1952, and *Freedom and Reason*, London, Oxford University Press, 1963.

For the development of communitarian theory in Germany and for the influence of thinkers of the Scottish Enlightenment on the thought of Hercer, Schiller and Hegel, see Plant, R., *Hegel*, London, Allen & Unwin, 1973, and Pascal, R., 'Herder and the Scottish Historical School' in *Publications of the English Goethe Society*, 1939, vol. xiv, p. 66. The British development of the idea of community is discussed in Williams, R., *Culture and Society*, London, Chatto & Windus, 1961. For the relationship of various aspects of community theory to theology, see Bright, L., ed., *The Christian Community*, Sheed & Ward, 1971, in particular the essay by S. Mews, 'Community as a sociological concept'; and Gilby, T., *Between Community and Society*, London, Longman, 1953: this book includes a discussion of theological views of community and society and also contains a discussion of the Greek polis as a paradigm of community. The communitarian nature of the Greek polis is also discussed in Sir Ernest Barker, *Greek Political Theory: Plato and his Predecessors*, London, Methuen, 1918.

3 The liberal community and community work

Some of the issues in the German tradition of communitarianism are discussed by Plant, R., in Cox, C. B. and Dyson, A. E., eds, *The Twentieth Century Mind*, (vol. ii, pp. 73 ff.), London, Oxford University Press, 1972. For a more liberal view, see Weil, Simone, *The Need for Roots*, London, Routledge & Kegan Paul, 1952. Social roles are discussed in Emmett, D., *Rules, Roles and Relationships*, London, Macmillan, 1966, and by Downie, R. S., *Roles and Values*, London, Methuen, 1971. A useful discussion of authority here is Peters, R. S., *Ethics and Education*, London, Allen & Unwin, 1966. Some of the issues of the American poverty programme are discussed in Lees, R., *Politics and Social Work*, London, Routledge & Kegan Paul, 1972. Elite theory is discussed admirably in Parry, G., *Political Elites*, London, Allen & Unwin, 1969. Some of the issues about human nature and politics are discussed in Duncan, G. and Lukes, S., 'The new democracy' in *Political Studies*, vol. xi, pp. 156 ff, 1963. Similar points reappear in Lukes, S., 'Alienation and Anomie' in Laslett, P. and

Runciman, W. G., eds, *Philosophy, Politics and Society Series III*, Oxford, Blackwell, 1967.

4   Human nature, community and the concept of mental health

Some of the issues about man's needs in the context of moral argument are discussed judiciously in Hudson, W. D., *The Is-Ought Question*, London, Macmillan, 1969. This book also contains most of the important papers on the topic. There is a rejection of Mrs Foot's and Professor Anscombe's views in Winch, P., *Moral Integrity*, Oxford, Blackwell, 1968. See also Norman, R., *Reasons for Action*, Oxford, Blackwell, 1971.

Bibliography

ALTIZER, T. J. J. (1967) *The Gospel of Christian Atheism*, London, Collins.

ANSCOMBE, G. E. M. (1958) 'Modern moral philosophy', in *Philosophy*, vol. XXXIII, 1958, pp. 1-19.

BACHRACH, P. (1967) *The Theory of Democratic Elitism: A Critique*, Boston and Toronto, Little, Brown.

BATTEN, T. (1967) *The Non-Directive Approach in Group and Community Work*, London, Oxford University Press.

BEDFORD, E. (1964) 'Emotions', in *Essays in Philosophical Psychology*, ed. D. Gustafson, New York, Doubleday.

BELL, C. and NEWBY, H. (1972) *Community Studies*, London, Allen & Unwin.

BERELSON, B. *et al.* (1954) *Voting*, Chicago University Press.

BONHOEFFER, D. (1961) *Sanctorum Communio*, London, Collins.

BONHOEFFER, D. (1962) *Akt und Sein*, translated by B. Noble as *Act and Being*, London, Collins.

BOSANQUET, B. (1917a) *Three Lectures on Social Ideals*, London, Macmillan.

BOSANQUET, B. (1917b) *Politics and Charity*, London, Macmillan.

BOSANQUET, B. (1917c) 'Philosophy and Casework', in *Social and International Ideals*, London, Macmillan.

BOSANQUET, B. (1923) *The Philosophical Theory of the State*, London, Macmillan.

BOTTOMORE, T. (1966) *Elites and Society*, London, Penguin.

BOWERS, S. (1950) 'The Nature and Definition of Social Casework', in C. Kasius, ed., *Principles and Techniques in Social Casework*, New York, Family Service Association of America.

CORGIAT, R. (1954) Article in *New Trends in European Social Work*, Vienna, Astoria-Druck.

COX, C. B. and DYSON, A. E. (1972) *The Twentieth Century Mind*, vols I, II, and III, London, Oxford University Press.

COX, H. (1968) *The Secular City*, London, Penguin.

CRICK, B. (1964) *In Defence of Politics*, London, Penguin.

CROSLAND, C. A. R. (1970) *A Social Democratic Britain*, London, Fabian Society.

DAHL, R. A. (1961) *Who Governs?* New Haven, Yale University Press.

DAHRENDORF, R. (1968) *Society and Democracy in Germany*, London, Weidenfeld & Nicolson.

DENNIS, N. (1968) 'The Popularity of the Neighbourhood Community idea', in *Reader in Urban Sociology*, ed. R. Pahl, Oxford, Pergamon.

DURKHEIM, E. (1952) *Suicide*, London, Routledge & Kegan Paul.

FOOT, P. (1958) 'Moral beliefs', in *Proceedings of the Aristotelian Society*, vol. 59 (1958-9), pp. 83-100.

FROMM, E. (1960) *Fear of Freedom*, London, Routledge & Kegan Paul.

FROMM, E. (1963) *The Sane Society*, London, Routledge & Kegan Paul.

GOODE, W. J. (1957) 'Community within a community—the professions', in *American Sociological Review*, vol. XXII, no. 2, 1957, p. 194.

HAMPSHIRE, S. (1959) *Thought and Action*, London, Chatto and Windus.

HEGEL, G. W. F. (1907) *Theologische Jugendschriften*, ed Nohl, Tübingen, Mohr.

HEGEL, G. W. F. (1927) 'Grundlinien der Philosophie des Rechts', in *Samtliche Werke*, ed Glockner, Stuttgart, Frommann.

HENDRIKS, G. (1972) 'Community development in Western Europe', *Community Development Journal*, vol. VII, no. 2, 1972. First published in *Development*, UNO, 1971.

HERAUD, B. J. (1970) *Sociology and Social Work*, Oxford, Pergamon.

HILLERY, R. (1955) 'Definitions of community: areas of agreement', in *Rural Sociology*, vol. XX, 1955.

HILLERY, R. (1968) *Communal Organisations*, Chicago University Press.

HOBBES, T. (1955) *Leviathan*, ed M. Oakeshott, Oxford, Blackwell.

HUME, D. (1964) *Treatise on Human Nature*, ed Selby Bigge, Oxford, Clarendon Press.

KARIEL, H. (1966) *The Promise of Politics*, New Jersey, Prentice Hall.

KARIEL, H. (1967) *The Decline of American Pluralism*, Stanford University Press.

KONIG, R. (1968) *The Community*, London, Routledge & Kegan Paul.

LEAVIS, F. R. and THOMPSON, D. (1933) *Culture and Environment*, London, Chatto and Windus.

LEES, R. (1972) *Politics and Social Work*, London, Routledge & Kegan Paul.

LEWIN, K. et al. (1939) 'Patterns of aggressive behaviour in experimentally created social climates', *Journal of Social Psychology*, vol. X, pp. 271-99.

MACINTYRE, A. (1964) 'Against Utilitarianism', in *Aims in Education*, ed T. B. Hollins, Manchester University Press.

MACINTYRE, A. (1967) *A Short History of Ethics*, London, Routledge & Kegan Paul.

MACINTYRE, A. (1972) *Against the Self Images of the Age*, London, Duckworth.

MANN, P. (1965) *An Approach to Urban Sociology*, London, Routledge & Kegan Paul.

MARCUSE, H. (1969) *Eros and Civilisation*, London, Sphere.

MARCUSE, H. (1972) *Negations*, London, Penguin.

MASLOW, H. (1957) 'Power Relationships and Patterns of Personal Development' in *Problems of Power in American Democracy*, ed W. Kornhauser, Detroit, Wayne State University Press.

MICHELS, R. (1958) *Political Parties*, Chicago, Free Press.

MILL, J. S. (1910) *Essay on Utilitarianism*, London, Dent.

MINAR, D. W. and GREER, S. eds (1969) *The Concept of Community*, Chicago, Aldine.

MITCHELL, B. (1971) 'Law and the protection of institutions', in *The Proper Study of Mankind*, Royal Institute of Philosophy Lectures, vol. IV, London, Macmillan.

MOSCA, G. (1939) *The Ruling Class*, New York, McGraw-Hill.

MOYNIHAN, D. P. (1969) *Maximum Feasible Misunderstanding*, New York, The Free Press.

NAEGALE, K. (1961) The 'Institutionalisation of Action', in *Theories of Society*, ed Talcott Parsons, Chicago, Free Press.

NISBET, R. (1960) 'Moral values and community', *International Review of Community Development*, 1960 (reprinted in his *Tradition and Revolt*, 1970, New York, Random House).

NISBET, R. (1967) *The Sociological Tradition*, London, Heinemann.

NISBET, R. (1970) *The Quest for Community*, New York, Oxford University Press.

PARETO, V. (1966) *Sociological Writings*, ed S. E. Finer, London, Pall Mall.

PARRY, G. B. (1964) 'Individuality, politics and the critique of paternalism—Locke', *Political Studies* XII.

PATTERSON, S. (1965) *Dark Strangers*, London, Penguin.

PETERS, R. S. (1966) *Ethics and Education*, London, Allen & Unwin.

PLANT, R. (1970) *Social and Moral Theory in Casework*, London, Routledge & Kegan Paul.

PLANT, R. (1973) *Hegel*, London, Allen & Unwin.

POPLIN, D. E. (1972) *Communities*, New York, Macmillan.

POSTON, R. W. (1953) *Democracy is You: A Guide to Citizen Action*, New York, Harper & Row.

POTTER, A. (1962) *Organised Groups in British National Politics*, London, Faber.

RAWLS, J. (1972) *A Theory of Justice*, Oxford, Clarendon Press.

RICHMOND, M. (1930) *The Long View*, New York, The Russell Sage Foundation.

ROBINSON, J. N. G. (1972) 'The dual commitment of social work', *British Journal of Social Work*, vol. 2, no. 4.

ROUSSEAU, J. J. (1964) *Oeuvres Complètes*, Paris, Gallimard.

SEEBOHM, F. (1968) *Report of the Committee on Local Authority and Allied Personal Services*, London, Cmnd 3703, HMSO.

SKINNER, B. F. (1969) *Walden Two*, New York, Macmillan.

SKINNER, B. F. (1971) *Beyond Freedom and Dignity*, New York, Knopf.

THOMASON, G. F. (1969) *The Professional Approach to Community Work*, London, Sands.

TIMMS, N. (1968) *The Language of Social Casework*, London, Routledge & Kegan Paul.

TIMMS, N. and MAYER, K. (1969) 'The clash in perspective between worker and client', in *Social Casework*, vol. XXXVI, no. 1.

TIMMS, N. and MAYER, K. (1970) *The Client Speaks: Working Class Impressions of Casework*, London, Routledge & Kegan Paul.

TÖNNIES, F. (1955) *Community and Association*, London, Routledge & Kegan Paul.

UNESCO (1951) *Democracy in a World of Tensions*, Paris, United Nations.

VATTANO, G. (1972) 'Power to the people' in *Social Work*, vol. XVIII, no. 1.

VERBA, S. (1961) *Small Groups and Political Behaviour: A Study of Leadership*, Princeton University Press.

WARREN, R. L. (1957) 'Towards a reformulation of community theory', in *Human Organisation*, vol. XV, pp. 8-11.

WEBBER, M. (1962) 'Order in Diversity: Community Without Propinquity', in *Cities in Space*, ed L. Wingo, Baltimore, Johns Hopkins University Press.

WHITAKER, B. (1968) *Participation and Poverty*, London, Fabian Society.

WILLIAMS, B. and MONTEFIORE, A. eds (1966) *British Analytical Philosophy*, London, Routledge & Kegan Paul.

WILLIAMS, G. (1972) 'Participation at neighbourhood level', in *Community Development Journal*, vol. VIII, no. 3, pp. 105 ff.

WILLIAMS, R. (1961) *Culture and Society*, London, Penguin.

WILLIAMS, R. (1965) *The Long Revolution*, London, Penguin.

WINCH, P. (1958) *The Idea of a Social Science*, London, Routledge & Kegan Paul.

WINCH, P. (1964) 'Understanding a primitive society', *American Philosophical Quarterly*, vol. I, no. 1, pp. 1.

WINCH, P. (1971) 'Authority' in *Political Philosophy* ed Quinton, Oxford, Clarendon Press.

WIRTH, L. (1957) 'Urbanism as a Way of Life', *Cities and Society*, ed L. Holy and A. J. Reiss, Chicago, Free Press.

WITTGENSTEIN, L. (1958) *Philosophical Investigations*, trans. G. E. M. Anscombe, Oxford, Basil Blackwell.

WITTGENSTEIN, L. (1969) *Blue and Brown Books*, trans. G. E. M. Anscombe, Oxford, Basil Blackwell.

WOLIN, S. (1961) *Politics and Vision*, London, Allen & Unwin.

WOOD, R. C. (1969) *Suburbia: Its People and its Politics*, New York, Houghton Mifflin.

YOUNGHUSBAND, E. ed. (1968) *Community Work and Social Change*, London, Longman.